Elite • 213

The Barbary Pirates

15th–17th Centuries

ANGUS KONSTAM   ILLUSTRATED BY GERRY EMBLETON
Series editor Martin Windrow

First published in Great Britain in 2016 by Osprey Publishing

PO Box 883, Oxford, OX1 9PL, UK

1385 Broadway, 5th Floor, New York, NY 10018, USA

E-mail: info@ospreypublishing.com

Osprey Publishing, part of Bloomsbury Publishing Plc

A CIP catalogue record for this book is available from the British Library

Print ISBN: 978 1 4728 1543 9

PDF ebook ISBN: 978 1 4728 1544 6

ePub ebook ISBN: 978 1 4728 1545 3

Editor: Martin Windrow

Map by Nick Buxey

Index by Zoe Ross

Typeset in Sabon and Myriad Pro

Originated by PDQ Media, Bungay, UK

Printed in China through Worldprint Ltd

16 17 18 19 20 10 9 8 7 6 5 4 3 2 1

Osprey Publishing supports the Woodland Trust, the UK's leading woodland conservation charity. Between 2014 and 2018 our donations will be spent on their Centenary Woods project in the UK.

www.ospreypublishing.com

ACKNOWLEDGEMENTS

The author wishes to record his gratitude to Dr David Nicolle and to Gerry Embleton for their generous assistance with illustration research. Similarly, his thanks go to galley warfare 'practitioner' Thomas Foss, who helped rekindle his enthusiasm for this subject and period.

ARTIST'S NOTE

Readers may care to note that the original paintings from which the colour plates in this book were prepared are available for private sale. All reproduction copyright whatsoever is retained by the Publishers. All enquiries should be addressed to:

www.gerryembleton.com

The Publishers regret that they can enter into no correspondence upon this matter

CONTENTS

THE BARBARY PIRATES
15th–17th Centuries

INTRODUCTION

For the best part of three centuries the Barbary pirates dominated the waters of the Western and Central Mediterranean, preying on the ships and coastal settlements of Christian Europe. From their heavily fortified bases on the shores of North Africa – the 'Barbary Coast' – their galleys and sailing vessels ranged as far as Greece, West Africa, and even the British Isles in search of victims. While they fought for plunder, their most lucrative activity was the capture of slaves. The slave-markets of Algiers, Tunis and Tripoli thrived on this steady traffic in wretched captives, and ensured that both the Barbary pirates and the emirs who ruled the Barbary states grew rich from the proceeds of human misery.

Calling these seafarers 'pirates' is perhaps a misleading over-simplification. The terms used for them are discussed below, but it is important to emphasize their essential nature as 'privateers', sharing their bounty with the North African ports that provided them with ships, men, and a ready market for their spoils. The Barbary pirates also served in the war fleets of the Ottoman Turks, and fought alongside them in many of the great galley battles of the 16th century, as well as in amphibious campaigns such as the siege of Malta (1565).

The 16th century was the heyday of the Barbary pirates, when their leaders rose to prominence as the actual rulers of Barbary states whose reach extended far beyond the bounds of the Western Mediterranean. The coastal city-states of modern Tunisia and Algeria were only nominally under Ottoman control; those in Morocco were independent of the Ottomans, and were usually only loosely controlled by the sultans in Fez. The Barbary states thrived on the profits of raiding and piracy, and their power extended into the African hinterland as far as the edge of that 'second sea' – the Sahara Desert. This study ends in the mid 17th century, when the European maritime powers managed to curb the most

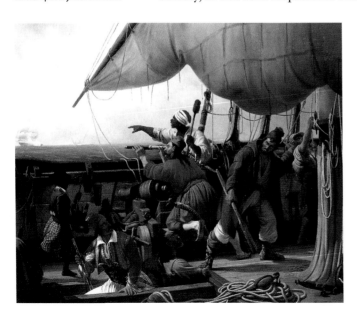

This lively 19th-century painting by an unknown artist shows Barbary pirates on the deck of a *xebec*, watching their consort attack a European sailing brig. Strangely, the dress depicted (apart from that of the Balkan soldier emerging from the hatch in the left foreground), may perhaps capture something of the 'feel' of the clothing worn by Barbary corsairs during earlier centuries, of whom there are virtually no contemporary illustrations.

damaging activities of the Barbary pirates through a combination of naval activity and diplomatic initiatives. From that point on, despite temporary resurgence during times of opportunity when European powers were distracted by major continental wars, it was clear that the great period of Barbary piracy had passed.

Nomenclature: 'pirates', 'privateers' and 'corsairs'

While most Christians regarded them as pirates, the predatory seafarers of the Barbary Coast were actually privateers: that is, in Western terms, seamen who had been granted a licence by a state to fit out a 'private man-of-war' to

This early 17th-century painting shows a Barbary pirate galley attempting to board a Spanish galleon. It faithfully reflects the narrow, crowded deck of the galley, with musket-armed janissaries stationed on the bow platform above the main guns. (Andreis van Eertvelt, 'A Spanish Engagement with Barbary Corsairs'; National Maritime Museum BHC 0747)

A view of Algiers from the sea, from an early 17th-century engraving. The inner harbour is invisible here behind the dark bulk of the fortifications on the islet christened Le Peñón by the Spanish, who maintained a garrison there from 1510 until 1539. Other forts guard the hills overlooking the city.

attack the shipping of the state's enemies. If such a captain captured a prize that was deemed lawful by the state's courts, then he could keep the value of the ship, her cargo, and – in the case of these Barbary captains – the crew as well, who were sold as slaves. In return, the state would get a share of the profits. A privateering licence or 'letter of marque' was only valid when the state that issued it was at war, and it only covered attacks on the state's enemies – but on the Barbary Coast the centuries-long religious conflict against Christian Europe was deemed an 'eternal war', so privateering licences were rarely revoked.

This continual state of maritime conflict was part of the greater 'Holy War' between Christians and Muslims, which by the early 16th century had been waged intermittently for the best part of 800 years. The 7th-century Arab conquests that began it were subsequently countered by the centuries-long *Reconquista* in Spain, and by the Crusades in the Middle East. After several hundred years of *jihad* and crusade the lands bordering the Mediterranean were fairly evenly divided between Christians and Muslims, but this balance would be altered by the Ottoman Turkish expansion from the east, and the Spanish and Portuguese continuation of the Reconquista into North Africa from the west. On the Barbary Coast itself this war did not involve huge armies and fleets, or great battles. It was a state of continual low-level warfare, involving individual privateering ships or small ad-hoc squadrons that attacked Christian ships, raided Christian coastlines, and captured Christians for sale as slaves.

The alternative term 'Barbary corsairs' is in fact more appropriate. It was current in the 16th century, when the Italian word *corso* meant the act of privateering, and a *corsaro* was an individual privateer – a sailor who made a state-sanctioned living from the *corso*. The term was also used by the French and Spanish, and effectively became shorthand not just for the Barbary pirates but also for Christian privateers such as the Knights of Malta. During later centuries the term corsair assumed wholly inappropriate romantic overtones, thanks to the hugely popular poem *The Corsair* (1815) by Lord Byron, the opera *Il Corsaro* (1848) by Verdi, and the ballet *Le Corsaire* (1858) by Berlioz. Today the terms corsair and pirate are largely interchangeable, which is misleading.

Even the term 'privateer' is not wholly appropriate in this context, since it implies that these sailors confined their attacks to the high seas. In fact they ranged all around the shores of the Western and Central Mediterranean, attacking from the sea to raid fishing harbours or other settlements within a few miles of the shore. Sometimes they ganged together into larger squadrons or even fleets, enabling them to threaten larger ports and communities. In this respect the Barbary pirates were similar to the 'buccaneers' who frequented the Caribbean during the 17th century. Those English, French and Dutch buccaneers combined attacks on Spanish shipping with raids on settlements in the Spanish colonies around the Caribbean basin, and in this the likes of Sir Henry Morgan were merely following the example set by Khizr Barbarossa two centuries before. However, today even 'buccaneer' is used as just another term for pirate, so for our purposes Barbary 'pirate' is as good a word as any.

The description 'Barbary Coast' is derived from the name of the Berbers, the warlike tribal people who inhabited (and still inhabit) the North African coastal region intermingled with the Arabs who swept in from the east during the first century of the great Muslim expansions. The original ethnic origin of the Berbers is still uncertain; it is claimed that 'Berber' derives from the Italian word *barbaro*, originally from the Latin *barbarus*, simply meaning 'barbarian'. By the 16th century the European term 'Barbary' had passed into regular usage as the collective name for the lands of the Berber people, so to insist on anything more pedantic here would needlessly muddy the waters.

Privateers and ports

As the pirates relied upon the small coastal states of North Africa for safe havens, recruits and resources, their fate became inextricably linked with that of the port cities that served as their bases. Soldiers recruited to guard the states' rulers took part in piratical raids, state arsenals supplied the pirates with ordnance, and in return the pirates helped defend the ports and their hinterland from attack. The fortunes of these 'rogue' states and the pirates who operated from their ports were closely entwined.

During the roughly 300 years of the 15th to 17th centuries, the 'eternal war' between Christendom and Islam was imbued with a fresh energy by, on the one hand, the aggressive expansion of the Ottoman Turks, and on the other by the efforts of Spanish-led Christian alliances to halt this Ottoman tide. Geographically the Barbary states, while allied to their fellow Muslims, were caught in the middle of this conflict. While this might have been disastrous for them, in fact they thrived, largely because Ottoman–Christian hostilities led to a dramatic increase in privateering activity. An influx of Turkish captains and Moorish émigrés to the Barbary Coast saw piracy as a way of taking the war to their religious enemies. The result was a long-running, low-level maritime conflict, with piratical attacks and slave-gathering raids playing a part in this greater religious

The slave market of Algiers: detail from a 17th-century European engraving illustrating a history of the Barbary states. In the right foreground a young Christian captive is being displayed by pirates to potential customers – Berber landowners, city merchants and (wearing a plumed turban) an *agha* of janissaries.

This detail of a mid 16th-century tapestry depicting the Spanish conquest of Tunis in 1535 shows Berber soldiers armed with short bows, guided (left) by a turbaned and red-robed figure, presumably an officer. This is probably a reasonably convincing impression of auxiliaries in Berber service during this period.

struggle. It should be noted that the religious confrontation was also complicated at times by separate alliances, which saw, for instance, Muslim corsairs aiding France against the forces of the Spanish and Italians.

HISTORICAL BACKGROUND

In AD 665 an Arab army marched westwards from Egypt into the *Exarchatus Africae*, the Byzantine province of North Africa. Two decades previously a similar incursion had secured control of much of modern Libya; this time, the Arabs planned to conquer the whole of the North African coast. The Byzantines were defeated outside their provincial capital of Carthage, and their influence was reduced to a small enclave surrounding the city. These conquered territories became the Arab province of Ifriqiya, which encompassed all of modern western Libya, Tunisia and eastern Algeria. By AD 698, when Carthage was captured, the Arab Abbasid *caliphs* ('commanders of the Faithful') based in Baghdad nominally controlled the whole North African coast from the Nile to the Atlantic Ocean.

They divided it into three provinces: Egypt in the east, Ifriqiya in the centre, and the subsidiary province of Maghreb in the west (stretching from the western border of modern Tunisia to the Atlantic coast, with its provincial capital in Tangier). For 2,000 miles, from Alexandria to Tangier, the peoples of North Africa were bound together by the secular power of the caliphs and the spiritual power of Islam. But while religious unity remained strong, any political union proved transitory. The subsequent Umayyad Caliphate ruled its North African provinces from Kairouan near Tunis, but in the mid 8th century a revolt in the west led to the establishment of independent Berber states across the Maghreb. In the 11th century one of these dynasties – the Almoravids –

RAID ON CORSICA, *c.* 1480

Corsica lay in the area of the Western Mediterranean frequented by privateers from Algiers, and here an Algerine galley lies off a small Corsican fishing village. Warned by lookouts in coastal towers, the inhabitants have fled into the hills, leaving the raiders free to search for plunder or any unfortunate villagers left hiding in their homes.

1: Barbary captain

This *Reis* wears a fur or fleece jerkin over his loose everyday clothes, and brandishes a *kilij*, the curved sword favoured during our period.

2: Bowman

Unlike the embarked Turkish janissaries of a generation later, the pirates carried whatever weapons were available and that

they were comfortable using. This seaman, based on a contemporary picture of Turkish archers, carries a short, powerful, recurved bow and a quiver of arrows, and has a sword slung from a baldric. He wears his jacket and shirt thrown back off his right shoulder for ease of movement in combat.

3: Berber crossbowman

This locally recruited pirate wears typical clothing of the Maghreb, and is armed with a crossbow with a composite stave, as used in north-west Africa for both hunting and war. Note the spanning hook on the front of his belt, and his straight sword with a plain cruciform hilt. The bow, quiver of bolts and spanning hook are based on examples in the Museum of Antiquities in Algiers.

Christian slaves dragging or carrying their chains as they go about their tasks for their Berber masters, in a 17th-century depiction of Algiers. These domestic slaves were fortunate: many others worked in the stone quarries, in the fields, or served as galley slaves. This scene is actually atypical of European engravings, which often depicted shocking scenes of cruelty in an effort to raise support for groups that were seeking to ransom Christian captives in the Barbary states.

unified these states and the Iberian province ɔ al-Andalus into one political entity. By the miɑ 12th century that dynasty had been replaced by the Almohads, whose caliphate was extended into Ifriqiya, creating a state that stretched as far east as Tripoli. Their rule lasted a century, before local revolts and Bedouin incursions led to its fragmentation and collapse. For the next 250 years, until the start of the 16th century, the North African coast was ruled by independent Berber dynasties.

The Hafsid and Marinid dynasties, 13th–15th centuries

In the early 13th century the Almohad province of Ifriqiya was governed by the Hafsid dynasty, but in 1223 the latter declared their independence from the Almohads, and thereafter they maintained their rule over the region from their capital in Tunis for another three centuries. During this period they extended their borders by absorbing the small neighbouring Berber kingdom of Tlemcen in what is now north-western Algeria, and by the 14th century their territories extended as far east as Tripoli. However, in the Maghreb to the west another expansionist Berber dynasty had established itself. These Marinids had taken power in Morocco in the 1240s, and within a century they were battling the Hafsids for control of Tlemcen. The zenith of Hafsid power was in the mid 15th century; after that their grip on the region was weakened by internal Berber revolts, Bedouin incursions, and attacks by the increasingly powerful Christian kingdoms of Spain and Portugal. Thus, at the close of the 15th century, there were two principal independent Berber states on the North African coast, both of them beset by internal and external threats.

THE FIRST CORSAIRS

Piracy in the Western Mediterranean existed long before the coming of the Barbary corsairs – indeed, predators had operated from ports along the Berber coast since the Vandals conquered the region in the 5th century AD. After the 7th-century Arab conquest such activity took on a religious element, as Berber raiders attacked Christian shipping and raided ports on the northern shores of the Western Mediterranean. During the medieval period pirates operated from ports on the coasts of southern Spain and Catalonia, from Corsica, Sardinia and Sicily, and from southern Italy. Beyond Italy, the Uskoks preyed on shipping passing their bases on the Adriatic coast of the Balkans, while Greek pirates operated from the rugged coastline of the Peloponnese.

What changed the situation on the North African coast was the late 15th-century climax of the Reconquista. The Spanish campaign of reconquest against Granada, the last remaining Muslim kingdom in Andalusia, led to a steady exodus of Moorish refugees to North Africa. The final capitulation of Granada in 1492 ended the Reconquista in Spain, but also ushered in a new ound of conflict as the victorious Spanish turned their attention to the ports of the African coast. During the 15th century the Portuguese had established a presence on the north-west coast of Morocco, capturing Ceuta in 1415 and Tangier in 1471. This gave them control of the southern shore of the Strait of Gibraltar, but they had little interest in expanding their North African possessions beyond the capture of smaller enclaves on Morocco's Atlantic coast – notably, Safi and Agadir – which served their greater focus on establishing trade routes around Africa and on to India and the East Indies. It would be the Spanish who would pose the greater threat, and their eastwards expansion along the North African coast would all but overwhelm the weak and divided Berber states that stood in their way. What the Berber rulers needed was the support of a powerful Muslim ally to halt this Spanish offensive.

The Ottomans

Following their capture of Constantinople (Istanbul) in 1453, the Ottoman Turks had pursued their own campaign of expansion. The collapse of the Byzantine Empire led first to the consolidation of Turkish power in Greece, and then to a renewed offensive aimed at driving back the forces of Christendom both in the Balkans and in the Eastern Mediterranean. While neither the Mamluks in Egypt nor the Ottoman Turks

One of the *Kuloghi* (a term meaning 'sons of slaves'), the force of auxiliary cavalry who served the rulers of the various Barbary states during our period. These horsemen were actually the sons of Ottoman officials who had married into Berber families. This arquebusier is clothed almost entirely in black (see Plate E4).

had been in a position to support the last Muslim rulers of al-Andalus with expeditionary forces, the Turkish Sultan Bayezid II had been able to offer help of another sort. He encouraged Turkish privateering captains to establish themselves in the Barbary ports, where they could support the Iberian Moors by harrying Spanish shipping, raiding the coast, and keeping open lines of communication with the remaining Moorish enclaves.

One of the first of these privateers was Kemal Reis, a Turkish captain who had spent the previous two decades commanding a band of privateers based on the Greek island of Negroponte (now Euboea). He arrived in North Africa in 1487 with a small squadron of *galiot*s, and established bases at Bougie (now Béjaïa) and Bône (now Annaba) between Algiers and Tunis. Kemal Reis led raids on Malaga and the Balearic Islands, and before the final fall of Granada five years later he evacuated thousands of Muslim and Jewish refugees from al-Andalus to North Africa. He was recalled to Istanbul in 1495, but many of his sailors stayed on in North Africa, their numbers augmented by vengeful Moorish exiles from Spain.

Unfortunately for the Berber rulers, continuing Ottoman support came at a price. Within a few decades the Ottomans would annex the North African states (with the exception of Morocco) and establish their own rulers – men who would defend their territories, but who owed their allegiance to the Ottoman sultan. The intermittent Spanish campaign of attempted coastal conquests, which lasted for the best part of a century, attracted the arrival of a new group of Turkish captains, who would first establish the fearsome reputation of the Barbary pirates. It was under their leadership that the Berber states would develop into a major thorn in the side of the Christian powers of southern Europe.

KEMAL REIS, (c. 1451–1511)

Kemal was unusual in that he began his career as an orthodox Turkish naval commander, and only became a privateer when ordered to support Moorish resistance to the *Reconquista*. In 1488, a year after arriving on the Barbary Coast, he embarked Berber troops and led a major raid near the port of Malaga, which had recently been captured by the Spanish. He duelled with Spanish coastal batteries, captured and destroyed Spanish shipping in several 'cutting out' expeditions, and took hundreds of prisoners. After 1492, reinforced with refugees from Spain, he led raids on the Balearic Islands, Corsica and the coast of Tuscany.

Recalled to Istanbul in 1495 to command a fleet in Greek waters, he spent four years reducing Venetian strongholds in southern Greece and Crete. This prompted a Venetian counterattack, and in August 1499 Kemal won a decisive victory in the battle of Zonchio off Pylos in the Peloponnese. He repeated this success the following year off Modon, leading to the Turkish capture of this key Venetian port.

In 1501 Kemal returned to the Barbary Coast, this time accompanied by his nephew Piri, who was a gifted cartographer. While Kemal led large-scale raids to Corsica and the Balearics, Piri Reis charted the coasts, and continued this work when Kemal extended his operations to the Mediterranean and Atlantic coasts of southern Spain. One of the prisoners taken was a seaman who had sailed with Columbus, and Piri's 1513 map incorporated what he had been told of the new lands beyond the Atlantic.

Kemal continued his forays against Christian shipping and settlements all over the Mediterranean until his death in a shipwreck in early 1511. His legacies were the integration of Moorish refugees from Spain into pirate crews, and a Barbary Coast which had grown reliant upon privateering.

The brothers Barbarossa

In the mid-summer of 1504 two Papal galleys were making their way south through the Tyrrhenian Sea, on a voyage from Genoa to Civitavecchia, a small port 50 miles north of Rome. The larger of the two was a *lanterna*, a flagship galley – one of the most imposing vessels of its day. Even its smaller companion was an impressive warship, with a powerful battery of forward-facing guns. Their crews did not really expect any trouble, so the captain of the lanterna was

surprised to see a small oared vessel appear from behind the island of Elba, and turn to face him in the 4-mile-wide channel between Elba and the Italian mainland. This stranger was a galiot, one of the small galleys favoured by the Turks and their new-found Barbary allies. It seemed no match for the two larger Papal warships, but it showed no sign of fleeing as the big galleys drew closer. In fact, the galiot's red-bearded commander, Oruç (or Aruj) Reis, had already ordered half his men to slide their oars overboard, thus ensuring that they could not retreat even if they wanted to.

Oruç and Khizr 'Barbarossa' (so named by Italian contemporaries, from their red beards). The brothers did much to turn the Barbary Coast into a pirate haven during the first half of the 16th century, and in the process helped to halt Spanish expansion in the area. After Oruç was killed at Tlemcen in 1518 Khizr succeeded him as *Beylerbey* of Algiers. His exploits over the following 28 years were too numerous to recount here (readers will find a detailed account in Ernle Bradford's *The Sultan's Admiral* – see 'Further Reading'). However, his most notable successes in the service of the Ottoman sultanate were his capture of Tunis (1534), his victory at Preveza (1538), and the reduction of Venetian settlements in Greece and the Aegean.

When the lanterna was a mile ahead of its consort, and unable to turn away, Oruç ordered his men to unleash a flurry of arrows; he then drove his smaller galley hard alongside the Papal vessel, and led his men straight up her side. Unlike the galiot, all of whose rowers were free men who joined in the fight, the Papal galley was crewed by slaves, chained to their rowing benches and unable to escape. Within minutes the lanterna's crew were either killed or overpowered, and Oruç Reis was in control of the ship. The Papal captain surrendered, then he and his men were led below into the galley's narrow central hold. If the rowers expected to be freed they were soon disappointed; instead, Oruç ordered them to turn the ship around. As his men dressed in the Papal crew's clothing and armour, a tow-rope was rigged between the bow of the galiot and the stern of the lanterna; then Oruç set off to capture his second prize of the day.

To the crew of the Papal galley it looked as if their flagship had just captured a pirate galiot. As the two ships closed most of the Turks hid below the bulwarks of their prize, and the rest pretended to be the crew of the lanterna. Once alongside, Oruç ordered his men to spring up and loose a storm of arrows onto the galley's deck. The second Papal warship was taken completely by surprise, and by the time the privateers swarmed aboard the fight was as good as won. An 18th-century chronicler of Algerine pirates wrote that 'The galley was instantly boarded and carried, with very little further bloodshed or resistance.' It was a stunning victory, and because the galleys were in the service of Pope Julius II it was one that caught the attention of Europe's Christian powers. It was clear that Christian mariners in the Western Mediterranean now faced a threat that was no longer confined to the waters off the North African coast.

After his victory Oruç Reis returned to Tunis, 250 nautical miles to the south – the white-walled port at the head of the Gulf of Tunis. Contemporary Arab chroniclers described it as 'the white, the perfumed, the flowery bride of the West' (less kindly writers would later call it 'odoriferous', thanks to the smell of the salt

DEFEAT AT BOUGIE, 1512

Even the Barbarossas were not always successful, and the fearless Oruç was prone to taking unwise risks. In 1512 the brothers were invited to help drive the Spanish from Bougie (now Béjaïa) between Algiers and Djidjelli – a substantial port fortified by the Hafsid dynasty. In preparation, Oruç had land carriages made for heavy guns captured on Christian ships; 1,000 janissaries were embarked along with Moorish exiles and local Berber troops, and the expedition sailed north from Djerba.

Arriving off Bougie in August, the force disembarked a little way from the city. The defences had been strengthened since the Spanish captured it two years previously, and new coastal batteries had been installed. Barbarossa's gunners bombarded Bougie for a week, and when a practical breach had been made Oruç led the assault in person at the head of the janissaries. They were met by a storm of artillery and small-arms fire; according to Haedo's *History of Algiers*: 'As [Oruç] was leading his men to the attack, a shot took away his left arm above the elbow.' The assault faltered, and the attackers withdrew carrying their grievously wounded commander. As the expedition headed southwards for home a fast galiot carried Oruç north to Tunis, where skilled Arab physicians were able to save his life.

The brothers' only consolation was Khizr's capture of a richly-laden Genoese vessel during his own voyage to Tunis, but the Genoese quickly took their revenge. A squadron led by the great admiral Andrea Doria took the Berbers of Tunis by surprise, and stormed La Goletta; the defences were destroyed and the village burnt, and a dozen Barbary galiots were carried off.

pans that ringed the city and of the stagnant lagoon on its seaward side). Oruç and his men were welcomed by cheering crowds, who realized that nothing like this had been attempted before. The Spanish historian Diego Haedo wrote: 'The wonder and astonishment that this novel exploit caused in Tunis, and even in Christendom, is not to be expressed, nor how celebrated the name of Aruj [Oruç] Reis was to become, from that very moment – he being held and accounted, by all the world, as a most valiant and enterprising commander. And, by reason that his beard was extremely red … from thenceforward he was generally called Barbarossa, which in Italian signifies "Red-Beard".' The dramatic career of the first of the great Barbary pirate leaders had begun, and in fact the renown of his nickname would be extended for decades by the fact that Oruç (*c.* 1474–1518) had a younger brother, Khizr (*c.* 1478–1546), who also became a privateer. Collectively they became known as the 'Barbarossa brothers', and they are generally regarded as being the two founding fathers of the Barbary pirates.

A romanticized 19th-century impression of Oruç Barbarossa leading the attack that put the Barbary pirates on the map of the Christian powers – the capture of a Papal *lanterna* in the summer of 1504. (Illustration by Leopold Fleming in Charles Farine's 'biography' of the Barbarossa brothers, *Deux Pirates*, 1869)

Like any that have been passed down the centuries in different tongues, the names of the brothers can cause some confusion. In Turkish Khizr was known as Hizir, but Hayreddin or Kheir ed-Din were also used, and even Hizir Hayreddin. For his part, Oruç is known as Aruj in the Spanish and Italian histories which are our major sources; in this book we choose to give the brothers' names in their original forms, Oruç and Khizr.

Oruç was born on the Aegean island of Midilli (now Lesbos) in 1474, the son of a retired Turkish soldier turned potter. Khizr was born four years later, and eventually the two became first seamen, and then Turkish privateers. In about 1490 Oruç was captured by the Knights of St John based on Rhodes, and spent about three years as a galley slave before the Turkish governor of Antalya (on the south-west coast of Asia Minor) secured his release. Oruç returned to privateering and it was claimed that he rose to command a group of galleys based at Antalya. He later returned to Lesbos, which he and his brother turned into a privateering base. By now both were seasoned commanders of some standing. It is unclear why they left their home region; one source has them travelling to Egypt in two galiots, and thence west to the Barbary Coast. Diego de Haedo claims that they went to Tunis independently, but it is more likely that they were sent by the Ottoman Sultan Bayezid II as part of his scheme to bolster the defences of the Barbary states.

In any event, they probably arrived in Djerba towards the end of 1502, leading a small force with two galiots. They set about conducting raids on the coasts of Sicily and the islands of Gozo and Malta, and while there is no record of it they must have been successful, since by the spring of 1504 they were invited to Tunis by the city's Hafsid sultan, Muhammed IV. The capture of the Papal galleys that summer was the brothers' first major success. When word of it spread, other Turkish privateers sailed west to join them, while local Berber warriors and seamen also joined this burgeoning pirate community. For the rest of that year and in successive cruising seasons the brothers roamed off the coastlines of Sicily and Calabria, garnering a lucrative crop of prizes, and prisoners to be sold in the slave-markets of Tunis. These successes encouraged yet more sailors to join them, while Berber and Turkish merchants alike proved increasingly willing to furnish the brothers with ships in return for a healthy share in the profits from the privateering enterprise. Rulers, merchants and corsairs alike were all winners, the only losers being their Christian victims.

CHRONOLOGY, 1450–1660

For geographical clarity, the modern names of Algeria, Tunisia and Libya are used here even though they did not then exist as states. The inhabitants of Algiers in our period are referred to as Algerines.

1453	Ottoman Turks capture Constantinople, renamed Istanbul; final collapse of Byzantine Empire.
1471	Portuguese capture Tangier.
1487	Arrival of Kemal Reis on the Barbary Coast.
1491	Moorish corsairs from Granada establish new base in Morocco.
1492	Moorish Kingdom of Granada conquered by Castile and Aragon.
1497	Spanish capture Melilla on Mediterranean coast of Morocco.
c. 1502	The Turkish corsair brothers Oruç and Khizr 'Barbarossa' arrive on the Barbary Coast.
1504	Oruç Barbarossa captures two Papal galleys off the coast of Tuscany.

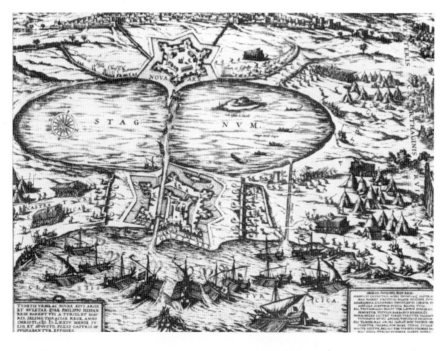

Looking from east to west, this 16th-century engraving of the capture of Tunis in 1535 shows the Spanish fleet supporting the siege of the Muslim defences on La Goletta (foreground, left centre). Behind it a dredged canal across the shallow lagoon (labelled 'Stagnum') leads to a new star fort guarding the approaches to the city of Tunis. In fact this fort did not exist; the city's waterfront bordered the western edge of the lagoon, and was only lightly fortified with a curtain wall.

The galley fleet of Khizr Barbarossa anchored off the French port of Toulon during the winter of 1543/44. At that time the great corsair leader was operating in French waters after the Turks and the French formed an anti-Spanish alliance. During the fleet's stay in Toulon the cathedral was even temporarily redesignated as a mosque so that they could conduct their prayers there. Note that the galleys are shown as all black except for light-coloured upperworks around the stern. (Detail of illustration in Topkapi Museum, Istanbul)

1505	Spanish capture Mers-el-Kebir on the Algerian coast.
1510	Spanish capture Bougie and Algiers in Algeria, and Tripoli in Tunisia, but their attack on Djerba island off the Tunisian eastern coast is repulsed.
1512	Oruç Barbarossa wounded in failed attack on Bougie, Algeria. Genoese admiral Andrea Doria attacks Barbarossa's base at La Goletta, Tunisia.
1516	The Barbarossa brothers gain control of Algiers.
1517	Oruç Barbarossa repulses Spanish attack on Algiers under Diego de Vara, and captures Tlemcen.
1518	Spanish besiege and recapture Tlemcen; Oruç is killed during a skirmish.
1519	Spanish assault on Algiers repulsed.
1522–23	Ottomans besiege and capture the stronghold of the Knights of St John on Rhodes. In recompense, the Holy Roman Emperor gives them Tripoli.

B GALLEY ARMAMENT, & BARBARY GALIOT, 16th CENTURY

Despite the wealth of information on a variety of strong, adjustable land gun carriages from as early as the 1470s, we have surprisingly little specific information about shipboard carriages in our period.

1a: A reconstruction, from archaeological study of the *Mary Rose*, of a cast bronze gun on a heavy, wheeled wooden carriage, c. 1530; smaller guns were mounted on simpler carriages. It is frequently suggested that those in the bows of oared warships had no wheels and simply rested on the deck, but unsecured heavy objects would slide around dangerously and be very difficult to manoeuver. Guns must surely have been securely fastened in place so that their recoil could be absorbed by the ship's timbers; we may be certain that 16th-century engineers were capable of designing efficient naval gun carriages.

1b & 1c: By the mid 16th century at the latest, galleys were mounting a large centreline bow gun firmly fixed in place, flanked on larger vessels by paired lighter guns and anti-personnel swivel guns. Obviously, the weights of all this ordnance had to be carefully balanced astride the centreline. These forward batteries on Barbary galleys were usually surmounted by a small fighting platform (arrumbada), where janissary archers, musketeers and boarding parties could take position. These examples are partly based on Guilmartin (see 'Further Reading').

2: Galiot

These small warships, well suited for privateering and coastal raiding, formed the bulk of the Barbary fleets throughout the 16th century. Their design was dictated by the need to accommodate two long lines of rowing benches and oarsmen, so any guns were necessarily mounted in the bow behind the spur or ram. The size of the battery varied, and smaller galiots typically carried only one centreline cannon. This image of a galiot seen from the stern is based on a surviving drawing by the Italian artist Raphael (d. 1520) and other contemporary references. Note the 'outrigger' support for the oars

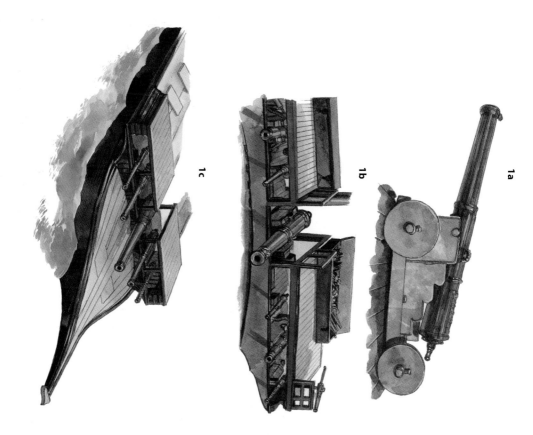

1a

1b

1c

2

At the great naval battle of Lepanto (1571) Uluç Ali commanded the left wing of the Turkish fleet, but withdrew his squadron when defeat was inevitable. This detail from a contemporary depiction of the battle captures the confused, close-range savagery of this type of galley fighting.

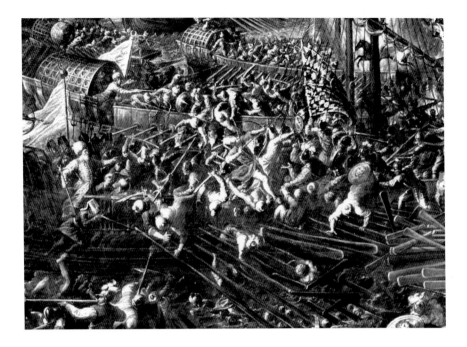

1529	Khizr Barbarossa captures Spanish fortress outside Algiers.
1530	Knights of St John re-establish themselves on Malta.
1533	Barbarossa is summoned to command an Ottoman fleet.
1534	Barbarossa captures Tunis.
1535	Spanish recapture Tunis. Barbarossa raids Minorca.
1536	French and Ottomans form an alliance.
1538	Holy League formed to resist Ottoman expansion. Barbarossa defeats Holy League fleet at battle of Preveza.
1541	Spanish attack on Tunis is repulsed.
1543	Barbarossa joins French to recapture Nice from Spain's Genoese allies, and raids Spanish coast around Barcelona.
1546	Barbarossa dies in Istanbul.
1550	Turgut Reis captures port of Mahdia in Tunisia, but it is retaken by Spanish. Andrea Doria defeats Turgut Reis at Tripoli, but he escapes to Istanbul, where the sultan gives him command of an Ottoman fleet.
1551	Turgut Reis and Sinan Pasha raid islands of Malta and Gozo, then recapture Tripoli.
1552	Turgut Reis and Sinan Pasha, with an allied French squadron, defeat Spanish–Italian fleet under the 86-year-old Andrea Doria off Naples.
1553	Turgut Reis assists French attack on Spanish in Corsica.
1555	Salih Reis and Algerines recapture Bougie.
1556	Turgut Reis installed as ruler of Tripoli.
1558	Turgut Reis raids Minorca.
1569	Turgut Reis and Piali Pasha defeat Spanish expedition against Djerba.
1561	Turgut Reis defeats Spanish squadron off Lipari Islands north of Sicily, and enslaves population.
1563	Algerine attacks on Mers-el-Kebir and Oran are repulsed.
1565	Unsuccessful Ottoman siege of Malta; death of Turgut Reis.

1568	Uluj Ali becomes ruler of Algiers.
1570	Uluj Ali captures Tunis, but Spanish continue to hold La Goletta.
1571	Holy League is reformed to counter Ottoman expansion. Ottomans defeated by Holy League fleet at battle of Lepanto. Uluj Ali is given command of an Ottoman fleet.
1573	Spanish capture Tunis.
1574	Uluj Ali and Sinan Pasha recapture Tunis.
1575	Spanish writer Miguel de Cervantes is captured by Algerine pirates.
1580	Spanish and Ottomans establish a truce throughout the Mediterranean.
1585	Algerine corsairs raid Canary Islands.
1587	Uluj Ali dies in Istanbul.
1601	Storm disrupts a Spanish attempt on Algiers.
1606	English pirate John Ward (Yusuf Reis) arrives in Tunis.
1609	Franco-Spanish raid on La Goletta.
1617	Barbary corsair raids on Atlantic coast of Galicia, northern Spain.
1618	Algerine fleet defeated by Dutch and Spanish fleet off Gibraltar.
1619	Salé privateers declare independence from Moroccan sultanate.
1620	Algerine fleet defeated by Spanish fleet off Cartagena, and Suleiman Reis is killed.
1621	Ali Bitchin becomes leader of the Algerine corsairs.
1622	Treaty between Algiers and the Dutch Republic.
1623	Treaty between Algiers and England. Death of English corsair Yusuf Reis.
1625	Salé corsairs ('Sallee Rovers') take shipping in Bristol Channel and off south coast of south-west England, and raid coastal villages: reportedly, 60 souls captured in Mount's Bay, and Looe burnt down. Shipping to and from Newfoundland Grand Banks hard hit, and fear of sailing damages fishing economy; mayor of Poole, Dorset, complains to Privy Council that in ten days some 27 ships and 200 persons had been taken by 'Turkish' pirates.
1627	Treaty between Salé and England. Murad Reis raids as far north as Iceland.
1628	Treaty between Algiers and France.
1629	French fleet bombards Salé.
1631	Murad Reis raids Baltimore, Ireland.
1637	English and French attacks on Salé and Algiers respectively: with agreement of Sultan of Morocco, William Rainsborough's squadron attacks Salé and frees some 300 captives. Ali Bitchin attacks French stronghold of La Calle (El Kala) on Algerian coast.
1638	Algerine and Tunisian corsair fleet defeated by Venetians at Valona.
1640	Renewed raids around Cornish coast; c. 60 captives reported taken near Penzance.

As the 17th century wore on, Europe's leading maritime powers – England, France and Holland – became increasingly enraged by the depredations of the Barbary pirates. This broadsheet demanded that the English parliament take action to free the roughly 1,500 English captives believed to be held in the Barbary states.

THE

CASE

Of many **HUNDREDS**

OF

Poor English-Captives,

IN

ALGIER,

TOGETHER,

With some Remedies

To Prevent their Increase , Humbly Represented to

Both HOUSES of

PARLIAMENT.

That there hath been taken, since their last breach with us , not less than an Hundred and Forty Sail of Ships and other Vessels, many of them being richly laden, besides the great Advance they make upon the persons they take, there being at this time upwards of 1500, (besides many Hundreds who have Dyed there of the Plague ,) who suffer and undergo most miserable Slavery, put to dayly extream and difficult Labour, but a poor supply of Bread and Water for their Food, stripped of their Cloaths and covering, and their Lodging on the cold Stones and Bricks; but what is more, their extream hard and savage lading them sometimes with great burthens of Chains, and shut up in noisome places, commonly adding some hundreds of blows on their bare feet, forcing out the very Blood, and sometimes on the Back, sometimes on the Belly, and sometimes on them all, insomuch that many are long decripit, some for ever, and some dying under their hands. But above all, is their frequent forcing of Men and Boys by their execrable Sodomy, also their inhumane abuses and force to the Bodies of Women and Girls, frequently attempting Sodomy on them also , some of whom both Males and Females have been so abused as hardly to escape with their Lives ; All which Usage is so notoriously known by those who have been redeemed thence, that it needs no proof.

First,

19

1641	Moroccan sultanate gains control of Salé.
1645	Death of Ali Bi□hin in Algiers. Report of 240 Cornish captives taken, though it is unclear whether at sea or in shore raids.
1655	English fleet under Cromwell's 'General at Sea' Robert Blake destroys Tunisian squadron at Porto Farina.
1659	Treaty between Algiers and England.

Relevant later events:

1662–84	Establishment of garrisoned English colony in Tangier.
1682–85	French punitive attacks on Algiers and Tripoli.
1704–08	English (British from 1707) gain naval bases in Gibraltar and Minorca.
1796	Treaty between Algiers and the United States.
1798–1800	French capture Malta, ending rule by the Knights of St John.
1801–05	Barbary War between Morocco, Tripoli and the United States.
1803–04	US frigate captured off Tripoli, then destroyed by US forces in punitive raid.

The bombardment of Algiers by an English squadron in July 1661, depicted here by the English mariner Edward Barlow, was thwarted by the strong defences of the port, which included a new fortified shore battery and a strengthened fort on Le Peñón (centre). After two hours the English squadron withdrew from the bay.

1815–16	Punitive attacks on Algiers, Tunis and Tripoli by British, US and Dutch squadrons.
1827	Ottoman naval power crushed by British, French and Russian fleets at battle of Navarino.
1830	French capture Algiers, and subsequently establish Algerian colony.
1881	French capture Tunis, and establish Tunisian colony.
1911	Italians capture Tripoli, and establish Libyan colony.
1912	Morocco divided between French and Spanish 'protectorates'.

 ACTION AGAINST A VENETIAN GALLEY,
c. 1540

Normally privateers tried to avoid tangling with Christian warships, but sometimes this could not be prevented; they might be escorting something valuable, or forming part of a Turkish squadron actively seeking out the enemy. Here the crew of a Barbary vessel are shown defending themselves against a determined boarding attack from a larger Venetian galley; the Venetians are clothed and equipped according to various Italian Renaissance paintings and extant examples in the Venice Armoury collection, and the Muslim weapons are based on those in the Algiers Museum of Antiquities. Contemporary paintings and prints show a huge variety of mixed arms and armour in use by common soldiers of this period.

The pirate Reis (1) probably wears ringmail or light composite protection beneath his loose, colourful outer robe.

He defends himself against the Venetian commander (2), who wears a light, partly gilded sallet firmly strapped in place, and half-armour of plate over a mail shirt. At centre, a well-equipped Berber musketeer (3) wears a turban untidily wrapped around the ubiquitous red cap, and a substantial mail shirt under his *burnous*; with no time to draw his sword or dagger, he tries unsuccessfully to defend himself with his discharged matchlock against a Venetian sword-and-buckler man (4). In the background, a Venetian musketeer (5) fires at point-blank range into the ranks of the defenders; over his doublet and hose he is protected only by a small steel skullcap helmet and an extended mail collar. In the foreground the unfortunate galley slaves, chained to their benches by the ankle, struggle amid the oars shattered by the Venetian ship's preliminary cannon-fire or the collision of the hulls.

THE BARBARY COAST

Cape St Vincent and nearby Sagres Point in Portugal, where Henry the Navigator established his centre for exploration, mark the south-west corner of Europe. Mariners should have felt reasonably safe here; after all, the bustling port of Cadiz lay an easy day's sail to the east, and the southern coast of Portugal and Spain was studded with harbours. However, from the late 15th century on, seafarers – especially Christian ones – took their lives in their hands when they rounded the two headlands southwards. Although the Strait of Gibraltar lay 170 miles away, they were already entering the home waters of the Barbary corsairs. The North African port of Tangier lay at the western end of the Strait, and from there, for more than 300 miles southward, the Atlantic coast of Morocco was dotted with pirate havens such as Salé/Rabat and Safi. From these the Muslim pirates could easily prey on ships rounding the twin capes, or passing through the Strait eastwards.

Once Christian mariners bound for the Mediterranean passed Tangier they had to run the gauntlet of the Barbary Coast stretching eastwards for 800 nautical miles until it reached Tunis – another great corsair haven. There the coast turned south beyond Cape Bon into the Gulf of Gabès, before turning eastwards again past the island stronghold of Djerba towards Tripoli. Beyond this last great Barbary port lay the Gulf of Sidra (today, the Gulf of Sirte), and a coastline that was largely devoid of harbours until it reached the north-eastern corner of the gulf and the coastline of Cyrenaica – after which Christian mariners ventured into waters controlled by the Ottoman Turks.

The coastline itself was almost perfectly designed as a pirate hunting-ground. Between Tangier and Tunis it was made up of a seemingly endless succession of small headlands, inlets and bays. In many places wooded mountains ran almost to the shore, giving lookouts excellent vantage points. A reasonably fertile hinterland supported enough agriculture to sustain the communities who made the coast their home, though studded with salt pans, small lagoons and rocky headlands. Dangerous shoals and shifting sandbanks made navigation tricky unless you knew the waters well. Beyond Tunis the coastline changed; apart from the small ports of Mahdia and Sfax, with one major exception the Gulf of Gabès was devoid of shelter all the way to Tripoli. The exception was the island of Djerba, one of the great havens of the Barbary pirates.

The Barbary Coast, showing the main bases of the 16th- and 17th-century corsairs. (Map by Nick Buxey)

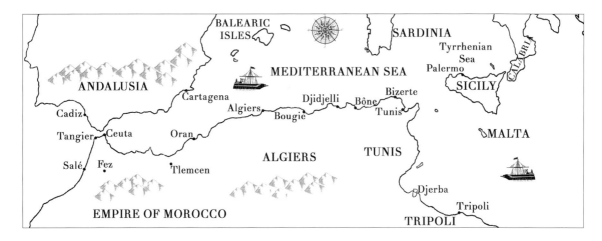

Herodotus declared that the island of Djerba was identified as Homer's 'island of the lotus eaters' where Odysseus was stranded on his voyage home from Troy. The largest island off the North African coast, Djerba was once a thriving ancient colony, but by 1500 it had become a backwater. It lay just off the mainland, to which its southern shore was linked by a shifting spit of sand. This enclosed the Boughrara, a lagoon large enough to accommodate a fleet, with only one narrow entrance at its north-western corner. This secure anchorage was of great value on a coast largely devoid of natural harbours, and where the highly changeable winds made navigation difficult.

Indeed, all along the Barbary Coast the winds could be dangerous. In winter northerly gales sprang up, blowing ships towards the African shore. In spring or summer a hot, sand-laden wind swept up from the Sahara Desert. Meteorologists call it the *sirocco*, but in Tunis it is called the *chili*; further east around Tripoli it becomes the *ghibli*, while in Egypt it is known as the *khamsin*. In its mildest form it is merely uncomfortable, but it can develop into a fierce storm. On at least two occasions during the 16th century Spanish fleets were caught unawares by these sand-laden gales, and many of their ships were lost.

Dotting this often capricious coastline were the great port cities of Tangier, Algiers, Tunis and Tripoli, and between them lay smaller ones such as Oran, Bougie and Bône. These were the centres of power in the region, where the local rulers and the Barbary corsairs maintained a symbiotic relationship. Away from the coast the belt of fertile countryside gave way to rugged mountains, and then to the desert. The coastal plain varies greatly in depth; in what is now Algeria it may extend 70–100 miles inland, but is slashed across with mountains that reach the coast; in Libya the desert runs right up to the shore, and fertility was limited to a series of oases and settlements linked by a dusty east–west road used by merchants and Muslim pilgrims alike.

Both geography and prudence favoured travel by sea. On land Bedouin tribesmen preyed on travellers in the east, while in the west Berber highlanders did the same. For a ruler in Tripoli, a trip to Cyrenaica took three weeks' travel by road, while the southern province of the Fezzan lay two months' away across the rocky desert. By contrast, the Christian island stronghold of Malta was just three days' sailing to the north. Throughout this period the sea was the main avenue of trade and communications; the coast was busy with the everyday shipping that linked its major ports, and other vessels venturing further afield.

This detail from a mid 17th-century Dutch map shows that mariners of that period were well informed about the basic geography of the Barbary Coast, identified as 'BARBARIA', even if relative distances are inaccurate. The second line of longitude from the right (actually, 10° E) is incorrectly shown as passing through Cape Bon, Tunisia, just across the unrealistically narrow straits from Sicily. At the bottom of the Gulf of Gabès the pirate lair of Djerba is labelled as 'I zerbi'. (From Joan Blaeu's *Atlas Maior*, Amsterdam, 1662–65)

The proximity of the Barbary ports to their Christian enemies meant they were all well-defended, often with fortifications that long pre-dated the risk of Christian attacks. Many of these settlements, including Algiers and Tunis, had been Roman towns, and had been fortified for centuries before the 'eternal war' began. By 1500 almost all of them had spilled beyond the bounds of their walls, and sat at the heart of developed hinterlands of suburbs and farms. At various times during our period these ports were captured by the Christians, and additional fortifications were established. In particular, the forts of Le Peñón at Algiers and La Goletta at Tunis were built by the Spanish to control these ports, and much of the campaigning between Spain and the Barbary states centred on these small but strategic island strongholds. For much of this period both the religious 'superpowers' of the Mediterranean – the Spanish and the Ottoman Turks – regarded the Maghreb as an arena in which to pursue their own ends; a series of invasions by the Spaniards driving eastwards could only be thwarted by Ottoman intervention on a similar scale. That the Barbary states survived was due not only to Ottoman help, and also to the enterprise and tenacity of their pirates.

THE BARBARY STATES

The small Berber states that played host to the pirates were independent from each other, and all functioned as feudal realms. With the exception of Morocco, any political entity's major port was its seat of power, and these were ruled and administered in similar ways. Each began this period as a Berber fiefdom, but during the 16th century all of them outside Morocco succumbed to Ottoman control. By the end of that century the cities' rulers were the commanders of either privateering fleets or of the janissaries – the Turkish soldiers installed in each regency to protect the ruler and the state.

In the early 17th century the small port of Salé on the Atlantic coast of Morocco became a hotbed of piracy. This 17th-century engraving of the place shows Salé on the left (north), separated from nearby Rabat by the intervening mouth of the river Bou Regreg.

Morocco

Morocco, in the west of the Maghreb, was the one significant exception to the pattern of development followed by the states of the Barbary Coast. This kingdom had long been an independent entity, and at its peak its influence extended into Spain. Now, however, it was on the defensive, beset by Christian invaders and unruly tribesmen. It also differed from the other states in lacking any major port. The Berber city of Tangier was held by the Portuguese, as

…arby Ceuta, and while they made no determined effort to venture …per into Morocco their presence deprived its rulers of a safe haven for …vateers on the Mediterranean coast.

The Berber Wattasid dynasty had ruled Morocco since 1472, when they wrested control of the country from the Marinids. Muhammad ibn Yahya ruled his newly won Moroccan sultanate from his inland capital of Fez, but he lacked the military muscle to repel the Portuguese. On his death in 1504 he was succeeded by his son Mohammed al-Burtuqali, who in 1508 launched an attack on Tangier. His assault was repulsed, as were two more over the next decade; the sultanate lacked the resources to oust either the Portuguese, or the new power in the region – the Spanish. In 1497 a Spanish army had captured Morocco's small Mediterranean port of Melilla as their first staging post on their drive eastwards along the Barbary Coast. Wisely, Mohammed al-Burtuqali left them well alone. (Remarkably, Melilla is still a Spanish enclave on the soil of the Sharifian Kingdom of Morocco, as is Ceuta).

The Christians were not the only threat to the Wattasid kingdom. The Arab Saadi family allied itself with the tribesmen of Marrakesh to the south, which gave them the strength to drive the Wattasids from power in 1554. The Ottoman Turks had backed the Wattasids, and in 1558 they sent an invasion force into Morocco led by the ruler of Algiers, Hasan Pasha (son of the privateer leader Khizr Barbarossa). However, after the inconclusive battle of Wadi al-Laban the invaders were forced to retreat, and the Saadid dynasty continued to rule Morocco for the remainder of our period. They proved slightly more adept at dealing with the Portuguese than their predecessors, driving them from several towns on the Atlantic seaboard; this campaign culminated in their victory at Ksar-el-Kebir (Alcazarquivir) in 1578.

This success brought the sultanate control of several small ports strung along Morocco's Atlantic coast. While there had already been some small-scale piracy, it was the expulsion of the *Moriscos* from Spain in 1609 that turned this into a major enterprise. Most of these Christianized Muslims went into exile in Rabat, just south across the Bou Regreg river mouth from the small port and privateering base of Salé. The Moriscos saw privateering as a tool for revenge, so piracy thrived there during the early 17th century. The Salé privateers (known in Britain as the 'Sallee Rovers') continued to be a major threat to trade, ranging deep into the Mediterranean, and in the Atlantic once even as far north as Iceland. Salé also attracted other pirates, including European renegades such as the Dutch-born Jan Janszoon (see below, 'The Pirates'). In 1624 he founded the Republic of Salé, which survived as an independent entity until its subjugation by the Moroccan sultanate in 1668.

Algiers as it was shown on a map of 1620 by the English mariner and cartographer Robert Norton. The city is ringed by walls, while a string of forts covers its landward and seaward approaches.

Algiers

Algiers was the largest and most populous port on the Barbary Coast between Tangier and Tunis, but it was never a significant pirate base before the Barbarossa brothers took control of it in 1516. In theory, Algiers formed part of the Hafsid Kingdom of

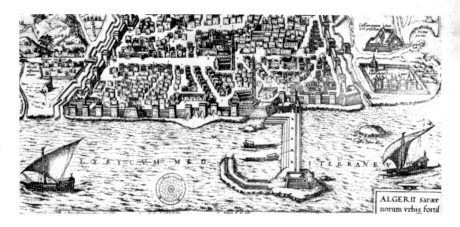

The inner harbour of Algiers was protected by a mole extending from the small islet of Le Peñón, using stone salvaged from the remains of the Spanish fort there after it was recaptured by the Muslims in 1539. Some of this stone was also used to build the small artillery fort on the islet, which anchored the seaward defences of the harbour.

Ifriquiya and was subject to the Hafsid sultans in Tunis. In practice, Algiers was ruled by the Emir Sālim al-Tūmī, who also controlled a hinterland extending as far west as the inland town of Tlemcen. A 16th- century Spanish writer described Algiers as 'a big city, well-populated, and surrounded by vast walls'. Another Spaniard, Jean Léon, recorded that the walls were strongly built using stone taken from the ruins of the small Roman town of Icosium which had stood on the site.

In 1516 Algiers had no thriving merchant community and no network of trading links. Contemporary Arab writers paid it scant attention, regarding the place as a pleasant backwater. Its harbour was sheltered by a small hammer-shaped island (named in Spanish Le Peñón, 'rock fortress'), which was joined to the city by a sandspit. As Algiers lacked a sizeable army the emir was unable to fight the Spaniards without outside help. In 1505 the Spanish captured the port of Mers-el-Kebir, and four years later they also took Oran; it was clear that Algiers was likely to be their next target.

The blow fell in 1510. First, the Spanish marched inland and captured Tlemcen; then they landed on Le Peñón and built a gun battery that commanded Algiers harbour. The island was fortified and a permanent garrison was established; effectively the Spanish now controlled the port, and the emir was obliged to pay a regular financial tribute to the garrison. This continued for five years, at which point Sālim al-Tūmī was forced to travel to Seville to pledge his fealty to King Ferdinand II of Aragon. This proved to be a humiliation too far: on his return in 1516 the emir sent a courier to the Barbarossa brothers, soliciting their help in driving out the Spaniards.

The Barbarossas were then based at Djidjelli (now Jijel), 150 miles to the east. While his brother Khizr stayed to supervise their privateering interests, Oruç set off for Algiers, but his intervention did not consist of driving the Spanish from their island fortress. Instead, it led to the murder of the emir in a coup, and with the help of 1,000 Turkish janissaries Oruç seized control of Algiers. The following year he defeated a Spanish force sent to capture the city, but he then relinquished control of his emirate and offered it to the Ottoman Sultan Selim I. This sacrifice of his autonomy in return for Turkish military support was well judged; but though it brought Oruç appointment as governor, he soon overreached himself.

In 1517, while Khizr raided the coasts of southern Italy, Oruç inflicted a costly defeat on a Spanish force that landed west of Algiers in May. For some reason its commander, Diego de Vara, did not throw up fortifications for his men and guns, and under cover of a sand-laden wind from the desert Oruç led janissaries and Moorish exiles at the spearhead of a shock attack that cost the Spanish some 3,000 killed and 400 captured before their galleys could evacuate the survivors.

Oruç then led a small army out of Algiers and headed into the hinterland, intending to secure control of the region to thwart any further Spanish landings. He seized Médéa to the south, then moved west to Miliana, before marching north-west to capture the Spanish-held port of Ténès; Khizr supported his brother by assaulting this port from the sea. Assured of Ottoman support, but without waiting for reinforcements to actually arrive, Oruç then marched on Tlemcen, 200 miles to the south-west. Since 1512 Tlemcen had been a Spanish vassal state; Oruç defeated its Zayyanid puppet ruler and captured the town. Early in 1518 the Spanish responded, predictably, by sending an army to recapture Tlemcen; during the siege that followed Oruç was killed, and the city was recaptured by the Spanish.

This could have created a power vacuum in the newly created Ottoman Regency of Algiers, but Khizr Barbarossa promptly stepped into his elder brother's shoes. He assumed the title of *Beylerbey* (supreme governor, or 'lord of lords' – a rank superior to *Bey*, 'lord' or governor). For the rest of his career Khizr, now the only 'Barbarossa', juggled his personal interests as a privateering commander with the duties of an Ottoman Beylerbey, and also (when occasion demanded) of an admiral of the Ottoman fleet.

Barbarossa strengthened the defences of Algiers, and with an influx of Turkish janissaries, artillery, ships and men he turned the city into a near-impregnable fortress. Nevertheless, it would be 1539 before his successors finally managed to capture Le Peñón. This obstacle had been avoided by anchoring ships or beaching galleys out of artillery range of its battery; small vessels berthed on the beach north-west of the city, while larger ships

This 17th-century engraving depicts a Spanish fleet arriving off Tunis. Although less than accurate, it captures the basic tactical geography of the place: the city lying on the far side of a large lagoon, protected in the foreground by the fortifications on La Goletta, the island linked to the mainland by a wide sandspit.

anchored in the outer bay. Barbarossa also built a customs house to control the landing of booty, an arsenal and a kasbah ('citadel'). After the capture of Le Peñón its walls were levelled and much of the stone was used to build a long mole, which greatly improved shelter within the harbour.

When Barbarossa left Algiers in 1533 he handed control to his *khalifa* ('deputy'), Hasan Agha. This officer successfully defended Algiers against a Spanish attack in 1541, but four years later he relinquished his title to Hasan Pasha, Khizr Barbarossa's son. After the death of his famous father in 1545 Hasan was replaced by Turgut (or Dragut) Reis, Barbarossa's gifted deputy. These successive rulers built Algiers into the largest privateering base on the Barbary Coast. In 1580, when the Spanish and Ottomans signed a peace treaty, the sultan downgraded the ruler from a Beylerbey to a Bey. Nevertheless, even after the golden age of the Barbary pirates had passed 70 years later the 'eternal war' would continue, and each spring Algerine corsairs would still set out in search of fresh prizes and a new crop of slaves.

Tunis

In 1504, when Oruç Barbarossa returned to Tunis with his captured Papal flagship, the city was ruled by the Sultan Muhammad IV, latest in a long

Spanish galleys and sailing ships – armed carracks – are shown bombarding the defences of La Goletta during the capture of Tunis by the Emperor Charles V in 1535. This is an unusually accurate depiction of galleys in action, with the masts stepped before going into action to reduce the risk of damage.

A fanciful 17th-century depiction of veteran Spanish soldiers scaling the walls of Tunis during the final assault in 1535. In fact access to the city was provided by Christian slaves, who rose in revolt and threw open one of the city gates just as the attack was being launched.

line of Berber kings of the Hafsid dynasty. While his family had ruled the region for the best part of 300 years, the sultan now faced a definite threat from the Spanish to the west, and a potential one from the Ottomans to the east. The Turks were poised to wrest control of Egypt from its Mamluk rulers, and it seemed possible that the Barbary states would be next. In 1504 Muhammad IV had been in power for a decade, during which he had greatly strengthened his city's defences and boosted the port's trade revenues.

Tunis was a thriving fortified city, set 6 miles from the sea at the end of a large, shallow lagoon. At its mouth was the city's main harbour, La Goletta (now La Goulette), sited on one of the two arms of land that all but encircled the lagoon mouth. Ships could cross the shallow lagoon by means of a dredged canal, and unload their cargoes directly beneath the city walls. This Goletta canal was dominated by a large tower called the Rades, built in the lagoon itself. Additional gun batteries covered the seaward and landward approaches to La Goletta, while a ring of marshy salt pans hampered any approach to the city's landward sides. Tunis attracted the admiration of travellers for the bustling industry of its port, its prosperity and its cosmopolitan markets, where merchants from most of Italy's city-states rubbed shoulders with Arab slave-traders. Before 1500 Tunis was not a major haven for pirates, but the arrival of the Barbarossa brothers and others like them gradually transformed it.

Tripoli viewed from seaward, in an early 17th-century engraving. Here the entrance was covered by a modern artillery bastion, while a string of rocks covered the direct approach to the inner harbour (left). This smallest of the three main Barbary ports was held by the Knights of St John from 1523 until 1551.

The Sultan of Tunis welcomed the arrival of the Barbarossas. A 19th-century history claimed that 'Aruj and his brother Hayreddin were kindly received by the king, who granted them free entrance and protection in his ports, with liberty to buy whatever they wanted. In return for which favour, the corsairs agreed to give him the tithe of all their purchases or booty.' After Oruç's success off Elba other prizes followed, and the number of corsairs based in Tunis grew. That attack inside the Tyrrhenian Sea had demonstrated that, unlike their small-scale predecessors, this new breed of pirates were willing to penetrate into waters that the European powers had previously considered safe. Such increasingly bold attacks attracted the attention of the Spanish, who captured Tripoli in 1510, but the Barbarossa brothers repulsed an attack on Djerba. Tunis now had two major Christian-held ports to its east: Tripoli, and Valetta in Malta.

Before the Spanish fleet arrived off Djerba the Barbarossa brothers had left Tunis to bolster that island's defences. This, and the brothers' subsequent moves to Djidjelli and then Algiers, did little to improve the safety of Tunis. When Muhammad Mulay al-Hasan succeeded to his father's throne in 1526 he did his best to improve relations with the Turkish sultan, but Suleiman 'the Magnificent' had already decided that the Hafsid ruler had to go. In 1533 Barbarossa was recalled to Istanbul; while his official task was to raise a fleet to raid Calabria the following year, he was also given another mission. In August 1534 he landed outside Tunis, captured the city, and expelled the Hafsid sultan. For a time Tunis was controlled directly by the corsairs; Mulay al-Hasan begged the Spanish for help, and the Holy Roman Emperor Charles V was happy to offer it. He gathered an armada of 76 warships and a fleet of transports, and in May 1535 he appeared off Tunis, landing some 30,000 troops and laying siege to the city. He concentrated on La Goletta, and after breaching the port's defences it was stormed and captured. Next, breaches were made in the city walls and, on 1 June, Tunis was assaulted and taken. Barbarossa escaped, but Tunis was now a Christian-held port.

Charles V returned Sultan Mulay al-Hasan to power, and he fortified La Goletta, turning it into an island fortress similar to Le Peñón at Algiers. However, the reign of the puppet was short-lived; Mulay al-Hasan had been an unpopular ruler before 1535, and now he was shunned by his own people. In 1540 his son Ahmad staged a coup, blinding and imprisoning his father. Three years later the deposed ruler was quietly killed, and Ahmad ᴖs proclaimed the new Hafsid sultan. In 1570 Uluç Ali, an Italian-born p ivateer commander and the newly appointed Beylerbey of Algiers, defeated Ahmad and captured the city, leaving the last Hafsid to seek asylum with the Spanish garrison of La Goletta.

In 1573 Don John of Austria, the victor of Lepanto, arrived off Tunis with a fleet almost as large as the one commanded by his father in 1534. He recaptured the city, but decided not to reinstate Ahmad; instead he appointed the Italian *condottiere* Gabrio Serbelloni as governor at the head of a Spanish garrison. The Turkish Sultan Selim II ordered Uluç Ali to recapture Tunis, and early in August 1574 a fleet of more than 200 galleys arrived off La Goletta. The Spanish withdrew to the island, but after three weeks of bombardment the fortress was forced to surrender. Until 1580 the government of the new Ottoman Regency of Tunis was supervised by the Beylerbey of Algiers. Subsequently lesser Beys governed the region, but from 1591 they were superceded by a self-appointed Dey – the commander of the city's janissaries. The Ottomans liked strong leadership, so these Deys remained in control of Tunis for the remainder of our period.

Tripoli

The least important of the great Barbary ports, Tripoli was still a bustling entrepôt where merchants from Europe, Africa and the Middle East gathered to do business. Founded by the Phoenicians, and later the Roman port of Regio Tripolitana, by the time of the Arab conquests it was known simply as Tripoli. The Arabs were taken by the beauty of the place, and called it Arūsat el-Bahr or 'Bride of the Sea'; in their turn, Christian traders called it 'the Mermaid of the Mediterranean'. In the early 13th century it had become part of the Berber Hafsid kingdom ruled from Tunis.

The port of Tripoli as depicted by the 17th-century Dutch maritime artist Reiner Nooms; several Dutch ships can be seen in the roads. After Tripoli was recaptured from the Knights of Malta by Turgut Reis in 1551 it served as a privateering base, but also as a trading centre visited by nations – like the Dutch – who had negotiated commercial treaties with the regency.

In 1510 the Spanish commander Pedro Navarro seized the city on behalf of King Ferdinand II of Aragon. The Spanish were repulsed from nearby Djerba, thanks to the actions of the Barbarossa brothers, but Tripoli would continue to be held by the Christians during the early 16th century. In 1523 the Emperor Charles V ceded it to the Knights of St John (or Knights Hospitaller) to compensate for the loss of their stronghold on Rhodes to the Turks the previous year. The Knights, subsequently based on Malta, held Tripoli and its hinterland for almost 30 years. However, they were unable to drive the privateers off Djerba, and in 1531 these pirates established a secondary base near Tajura just 10 miles east of Tripoli. The catalyst for their final eviction came in 1550, when the great Genoese commander Andrea Doria arrived off Djerba, trapping the fleet of Turgut Reis inside its lagoon. Turgut escaped by dragging his galleys across the sandspit joining the island to the mainland, and made his way to Istanbul, where Suleiman the Magnificent gave him command of a Turkish fleet.

In early August 1551, after capturing and sacking Gozo, Turgut arrived off Tripoli once again; he landed an army of several thousand janissaries, and began bombarding the port. After two weeks the mutinous garrison demanded that their commander, Gaspard de Vallier, surrender. This he did on 15 August, but while he was released, his knights were sold into slavery. Turgut installed Ağa Murat, the commander of Tajura, as the new governor of Tripoli, but by the end of the year Sultan Suleiman named Turgut himself as the Bey – a post he held for five years until he was given the grander title of Pasha of Tripoli. Under Turgut's rule Tripoli became a privateering port, with rebuilt and strengthened defences. After his death in 1565 the regency changed hands several times, but Tripoli remained an Ottoman province, and continued to provide a safe haven for Barbary pirates until the 19th century.

THE SHIPS

The galiot
When Oruç Barbarossa captured the Papal flagship and its consort in the summer of 1504, the vessel he used was a *galiot* (or *galliot*). While the term was used to describe other types of vessel in the 17th and 18th centuries, the galiot used by Oruç was quite clearly defined. Essentially it was a small galley, with just 16 to 20 oars on a side, and usually 18. During this period galleys of various types were almost always classified by the numbers of oars or rowing benches on each side, and the number of oarsmen manning each oar. There was some degree of cross-over in these categories, but essentially the larger a vessel the more men pulled each oar. Larger galiots did exist, some being as large as normal-sized galleys, but unlike the galley, which always had more men on each oar, the smaller galiot was always rowed *alla scaloccio*, with two rowers per sweep.

These craft also sat lower in the water than galleys, and consequently had a lower freeboard. While this made them less suitable for long open-water voyages, they made up for it by having a very favourable power-to-weight ratio – i.e., their relatively small displacement made them faster and more manoeuvrable than larger oared vessels. They carried a single mast fitted with a large lateen sail – a triangular rig that allowed the vessel to sail close into the wind. While no dimensions of Barbary galiots have survived, Venetian shipbuilding sources reveal that a typical example of the first half of the 16th century, measured in Venetian *braccios*, was 18½ long, 2 across the beam, and with a draft of just over 1⅓ braccios without ordnance, spars or masts. This equates to 27 metres (88½ feet) in overall length, including a spur at the bow; 3m (9¾ft) wide; and 2m (6½ft) in the draft. This lack of water resistance, combined with a healthy suite of oars, was the key to the speed and agility of these vessels. The Venetians recorded that their average 18-bank galiot (i.e., with 18 benches per side) carried 72 oarsmen, supported by 10 gunners and up to 60 marine soldiers. Some contemporary descriptions of Barbary galiots in action mention crews of as many as 200, although this would have made these craft dangerously overmanned for normal navigation. For longer-range voyages, where every square metre was precious, crews cannot have been dissimilar to the totals given by the Venetians.

This depiction of a Barbary galiot, in a detail from a 17th-century painting by Lieve Pietersz Verschuir, may have an exaggeratedly raked bow and overhanging stern, but the proportions of the vessel reflect contemporary descriptions. Note that the artist depicts the hull as black and all upperworks and the oars as red.

This Venetian woodcut depicting the battle of Zonchip (1499) shows small Turkish galiots engaging Venetian armed carracks. The scene is interesting in its depiction of the boarding tatics employed by the Turks, and also provides us with a rare depiction of Kemal Reis (centre, labelled 'Chmali'), the Ottoman naval commander who pioneered the use of privateers based on the Barbary Coast.

Armament invariably consisted of a single large gun mounted on the centreline of the ship in the bow. This would be a bronze weapon, possibly of Turkish manufacture, a captured weapon, or one cast in the small foundry in Tunis. It would have fired a 12- to 24-pound ball (5.4–11.8kg), with 16-pdrs (7.25kg shot) being the most common guns. By the later 16th century some of the larger galiots appeared with two smaller flanking guns mounted in the bow, usually 6- or 8-pdr weapons. All vessels also carried a number of light swivel-mounted pieces on top of their bow gun platform, capable of firing either 1-pdr (0.45kg) balls, or bags of 'dice shot' – musket balls or small scraps of stone or metal. While the larger gun was primarily to fire into the hull of the enemy ship, these swivel guns were purely anti-personnel weapons, to sweep an enemy's deck immediately before the pirates boarded.

The galley

While galiots remained the Barbary pirates' vessel of choice throughout the 16th century, galleys were also used in significant numbers. A typical galley of that period carried 20 to 25 oars per side, in a single line – the more oars, the longer the vessel. While other maritime powers experimented with a different rowing system powered by more men, the Barbary pirates and Ottoman Turks kept to their own version of the *alla sensile* system, with three men serving each oar. This gave a typical 24-bank Barbary galley a crew of 144 oarsmen, which tallies with Turkish manning accounts of the period. A galley of this size would also carry around 20 gunners and 80 to 100 soldiers.

In addition to its large centreline gun it would carry at least one and sometimes two smaller pieces mounted on either side of it, in a similar fashion to the larger galiots. The only difference was that the greater size of the vessel permitted the employment of heavier guns, with centreline calibres of up to 36 pounds, and flanking guns of up to 18 pounds. A 24-bank *galia sotil* (ordinary galley) of the early 16th century was, according to Venetian treatises, the equivalent of 41m (134½ft) long, with a 5m (16½ft) beam, and a draft of 1.5m (5 feet). Typically, a galley of this size had a displacement of approximately 200 tons. They usually carried two masts, each fitted with a lateen sail. While the power-to-weight ratio might have been inferior to that of a galiot, these vessels made up for it with their greater fighting potential. There is no indication that the Barbary pirates made use of larger flagship galleys – *sultanas* or *lanternas* – during this period, except when these vessels formed part of an Ottoman fleet and were crewed by Turkish mariners.

The *fusta* and *barca longa*

A much smaller oared vessel occasionally used by pirates was the *fusta*. These had 10 to 15 oars per side, each served by two men, and carried a single small centreline gun (if any were carried at all, other than swivel pieces). With a crew of 60 oarsmen and about 30 soldiers, these craft were considered too small to participate in major engagements, and they also lacked the iron-shod spurs fitted to most galiots and galleys for ramming. However, they were suitable for short-range raiding and for scouting. A typical fusta was a little over 20m (65½ft) long, and was fitted with a single mast and lateen sail.

A variant favoured by the Barbary pirates was the *barca longa*. (Some European writers described these vessels as *begantines* – a term applied to a range of ship types, as its definition evolved throughout the age of sail.) A barca longa had a similar number of oars to a fusta, but each was pulled by just a single rower. Their limited range made them unsuitable for operations far from the coast, but they were perfectly designed for darting out and attacking a passing ship before it could escape. While typically they could carry a crew of 20–30 oarsmen and 20 soldiers the numbers could be increased for short periods.

This slightly odd 17th-century European depiction of a pirate galley shows the stern as too massive and stately, belied by contemporary descriptions of these low, fast vessels. Nevertheless, it is interesting for its faithful depiction of the rig of the galley's single lateen sail, and its impression of the fighting crew packed on the central deck between the rowing benches.

This contemporary depiction of a Barbary or Ottoman Turkish galley, and a smaller galiot beyond it, shows many flags in dark red, black, green and white; contemporary Christian accounts speak of pirate galleys festooned with taffeta and silk banners. Note that the oars are shown as red, the masts and spars greenish-blue, and the canopy over the poop as a Turkish 'carpet' design on a red ground.

One great advantage enjoyed by the Barbary pirates was that for the most part their smaller galiots and fustas were manned by free men, and barca longas were exclusively crewed by free volunteers. This meant that (as demonstrated in the action between Oruç Barbarossa and the Papal flagship) when the ships came alongside, the oarsmen could pick up a weapon and join in the fight. This gave them a useful edge in boarding actions, and allowed these small craft to 'punch above their weight'.

The *xebec*

While the romanticized view of the Barbary pirates is that they almost exclusively used oared warships, the truth is that they also employed the types of sailing vessels that had operated out of the Barbary ports for

POLACCA & TARTANS

These craft are typical of the types that frequented Barbary Coast ports during the 16th and 17th centuries, being employed for both commerce and privateering. Their everyday appearance helped deceive potential victims into identifying them as harmless merchantmen or fishing boats until it was too late to escape a sudden attack.

1 & 2: Tartans

These were small coastal craft with a single small mast and a lateen sail augmented by a jib. They were rarely armed, and if at all with nothing more than a pair of swivel guns mounted on the gunwales. Such craft were employed to dart out from hiding-places along the coast and attack a passing ship before it could escape. These two slightly differing rigs for the lateen sail and jib were both commonplace during our period.

3: Polacca

These three-masted sailing vessels used lateen sails throughout the 16th century, but pictorial evidence

suggests that as the 17th century wore on combinations of lateen and square rig became common, giving them versatility in the highly changeable wind conditions encountered off the North African coast. This example has a square-rigged course (mainsail), topsail and topgallant on its mainmast; a lateen sail on its foremast; and a square topsail above a smaller lateen on its mizzen. It has only one pierced broadside gunport, the smaller holes being scuppers. More guns could be mounted if needed, but the fewer were visible, the better the chances of being mistaken as harmless.

4: Small craft

Even smaller boats were also employed by privateers for various purposes, including towing sailing vessels when they were becalmed, or approaching anchored craft surreptitiously by night. Many had the curved hull shape still seen in the Mediterranean.

centuries. Some of these were powered by both sail and oar. While this al·o applied to galleys of various sizes, those were primarily designed to ·e propelled by oars, using sail only in favourable wind conditions and never in combat. By contrast, these other vessels were primarily sailing ships, which retained some ability to be propelled by oars in light winds or when becalmed. The influx of European renegades in the early 17th century led to an increase in the use of sailing vessels as privateers. These desperadoes brought with them expertise in the operation of square-rigged craft, and an amalgam of their experience with traditional Barbary designs proved a successful combination.

The largest and most powerful of these sail-powered ships was the *xebec*. This was a slim, fast-looking vessel, with an elegant and rakish overhang at the bow and the stern. While the hull at the waterline was noticeably narrow, it widened out as it rose so that the upper deck was surprisingly beamy. This was a three-masted vessel, usually rigging large triangular lateen sails on all three masts. Later in the 17th century some began to appear with a combination of lateen and more conventional square sails, of the kind used in northern Europe. This was achieved by hauling down the spar used for a lateen sail and hoisting up a new spar suitable for a square-rigged sail. More commonly, however, the lateen sails were left where they were, and square topsails were hoisted on smaller square-rig spars. This combination meant that, in the right hands, these craft could sail closer to the wind than most square-rigged European merchant ships, but could also take advantage of wind conditions that favoured square sails. By the very end of our period, in the late 17th century, the lateen sail on the mainmast was sometimes replaced by two or three square-rigged spars, carrying a square mainsail or course, a topsail and a topgallant. This development was, of course, due to the influence of the European renegades. However, for most of our period, and in most cases, a Barbary xebec would simply carry three lateen-rigged sails.

The larger Barbary xebecs were typically about 30–35m (98–114ft) long, with a 6–8m (20–26ft) beam. They had a row of oar ports in their hull sides, so sweeps or oars could be used if the occasion demanded. This, and the potential array of sails it could carry, gave a Barbary xebec an impressive degree of flexibility. In most cases these ships carried between 12 and 16 guns, half of them in each broadside or with some repositioned to serve as bow chasers. The usual swivel guns were also fitted along the gunwales.

The *polacca*

The *polacca* might appear, to a landsman, to be virtually identical to the xebec. Both had three masts and generally similar-shaped hulls, but the polacca, though rigged with a combination of lateen and square sails, lacked the xebec's versatility. It carried lateen sails on the mizzen mast and foremast, but in most cases the mainmast was designed to carry nothing but three square sails – a course, a topsail and a topgallant. Some also carried square topgallants above the lateen sails on the foremast and mizzen mast, but unlike the case with the xebec these were permanently rigged; the distinction is that a polacca did not carry a combination of lateen and square sails for selective use depending on wind conditions.

The other major difference was that polaccas were generally broader beamed at the waterline than xebecs, since they were designed primarily to carry cargo. This made them slightly slower, but under a full press of sail, and in most conditions, they could still overtake most European merchant ships. Another distinction was that the polacca was not fitted with oar ports, so lacked the xebec's ability to attack a becalmed enemy. Generally, polaccas were smaller and less well armed than xebecs, carrying four to eight guns as well as swivel pieces.

The *felucca* and *tartan*

The *felucca* was a small one- or two-masted vessel used throughout the Mediterranean, but particularly favoured by the Barbary pirates. Like a xebec, a felucca had a narrow beam, and it also boasted the elongated stem which was a distinctive feature of the larger xebec. While it lacked the ability to replace its two triangular lateen sails with square-rigged ones, it did have oar ports – usually between three and six per side, but some of the larger feluccas of the late 17th and early 18th centuries had up to 16 per side. However, in our period a felucca was more of a sailing than an oared craft, and its narrow hull and good power-to-weight ratio gave it useful speed. While a felucca did not normally carry guns other than a couple of swivel pieces, it was an ideal craft from which to launch a sudden boarding attack. Even smaller vessels were also used on occasion. The *tartan* was a small lateen-rigged Mediterranean fishing vessel; in the hands of pirates they were unobtrusive, and a number of them could be mistaken for a

While the use of Barbary galleys and galiots continued in the 17th century, an increasing use was made of sailing craft. These came in a variety of designs and sizes, but this ship-rigged three-masted privateer is one of the larger ones. (Original painting by Andries van Ertvelt)

fishing fleet until they launched themselves against an unsuspecting victim. Usually no more than 15m (50ft) long, they carried a single mast fitted with a small lateen sail, as well as a jib running between the mast and a bowsprit. The tartan lacked the speed of the barca longa, and could hold no more than about 30 men.

'Roundships'

At the other end of the spectrum was the three-masted 'roundship' or *carrack*. This was the archetypal northern European ship of the Renaissance period, which could be employed either as a merchantman or a warship. With high sides, they were difficult to board from galleys or smaller craft, and what they lacked in speed they made up for in their ability to mount broadsides of guns. While such vessels were not used by the Barbary pirates before the 17th century, the later influx of European renegades created a large pool of seamen with the experience to handle them, so if one was captured it might be pressed into service as a privateer. There are even accounts of renegades bringing roundships with them to the Barbary ports, either after a mutiny or having captured one at sea en route. This underlines the fact that by the late 17th century the corsairs had vessels at their disposal to suit every purpose.

The imposing figure of Ali V Ben-Ahmed, (or Ali Khoja), a late 18th-century ruler of Algiers, depicted surrounded by the severed heads of his enemies. While out of our period, this stands for the caricatured Western image of Barbary rulers: cruel, despotic and self-indulgent. In fact many were experienced sea-captains, and their rule was often perceived as efficient and just by contemporary Muslim standards.

THE PIRATES

The Barbary pirates were a surprisingly organized group, with a command structure that promoted skill and performance, and one that was closely integrated with the governance of the state where the corsairs were based. The same basic system remained in place throughout the 16th and 17th centuries, both in terms of the way the ships were run, and the manner in which the state's administrative system was designed to support privateering operations. The result was a well-integrated organization that varied little from one

BARBARY *XEBEC*, EARLY 17th CENTURY

Typical of the small privateering sailing vessels operating out of the Barbary ports, the *xebec* was a three-masted design with a pronounced rake at bow and stern, and a notably narrow beam at the waterline which gave fast sailing lines. Traditionally they were lateen-rigged, but as the 17th century progressed they tended to carry spare spars so that they could haul up square sails if conditions demanded, and a row of oar ports allowed the crew to use sweeps (here carried aft) if they were becalmed. Although the craft illustrated is a small example, little more than 25 metres long, the surprisingly beamy deck allows it to mount a substantial broadside of at least eight to ten 4-pdr or 6-pdr guns, plus pairs of swivels on the gunwales. They could usually overhaul most contemporary merchantmen, and their crews, several dozen strong, could usually overcome any resistance when they boarded. To encourage early surrender the plain black flag sends the corsairs' message: 'No quarter!'

Officials working for a Barbary ruler are shown negotiating payment for the purchase of Christian slaves by the Redemptionist Fathers. The Muslim states did not allow religious hostility to stand in the way of commerce; to them slaves were a commodity like any other, and if the price was right they had no objection to allowing Christians to buy back their co-religionists.

Barbary state to another, particularly after the three main states were assimilated into the Ottoman Empire as the Algiers, Tunis and Tripoli regencies.

Chain of command in the Ottoman regencies

First, the Ottoman sultan issued a *firman* ('royal decree') appointing a ruler to govern one of his Barbary provinces. This governor might hold the rank of Pasha, Beylerbey or Bey (in descending seniority), and his initial appointment was usually for three years, after which it could be extended or cancelled. The sultan expected the obedience of the ruler, particularly in matters of foreign policy; an annual financial tribute to Istanbul; and to be provided with ships and men for his fleets when they were demanded. Otherwise the ruler was given a surprisingly free hand to govern his territory as he saw fit.

The ruler would be guided by a *divan* – a council of local notables – while another council known as a *taiffa* advised him in naval or privateering matters. This taiffa consisted of the port's senior privateering captains, led by the regency's *Capudan Pasha* or local admiral (sometimes known as the 'Reis of the Marine'). This direct access to the ruler gave the privateering captains considerable influence in the regency. For military matters the ruler was advised by a *Bey de Camp*, usually the commander of his janissaries, whose duties included the annual collection of taxes as well as ensuring the security of the regency. The *Grand Kehya* ('chamberlain') controlled the administration of the regency, and also chaired meetings of the divan. Meanwhile the chamberlain's deputy supervised foreign affairs, and also the kasbah guards, who for security reasons were not under the control of the Bey de Camp. Other lesser officials oversaw various aspects of the regency's administration, including the operation of the slave-markets, trade within the regency and the policing of the city. As the regency's legal framework was based on the *Sharia*, the ruler was advised by a *mufti*, and justice was usually swift and severe. In theory the same draconian system applied on the regency's ships and privateers when they were at sea; in practice, however, the Capudan Pasha, the taiffa and individual captains were largely left to govern their own affairs.

Strangely, while the original holders of the title of Capudan Pasha were usually Turks or leading local privateers, by the 17th century the post was frequently held by a European renegade. The Capudan Pasha had a headquarters building near the harbour, and from there he and a small staff of clerks supervised the movement of all merchant shipping, as well as the activities of privateers and any regency warships. Before a privateering captain could put to sea he had to obtain permission to sail from the Capudan Pasha, and collect a renewed 'letter of marque' from the taiffa. This council established cruising areas in advance, and often the duration of cruises. If the vessel was a galley or galiot, however, the lack of space for water, provisions, captives or plunder naturally meant that cruises were of fairly short duration. Once these permissions were granted the captain hoisted a green flag at his masthead to indicate that he was about to sail on a *corso*, and his crew would embark, accompanied in many cases by a detachment of the regency's janissaries.

The captains

The *reis* ('captain') was chosen by the ship's owners, although candidates also had to be approved by the taiffa and the Capudan Pasha. The origins of privateering captains varied considerably. In the early 16th century the large majority of them were Turks – though that catch-all term included seamen from Greece, the Balkans, Syria, Egypt, or elsewhere in the Eastern Mediterranean as well as the Turkish heartland of Asia Minor. At first very few were Berbers, although a number of North African seamen did rise to prominence during the 16th century. Others were Moorish exiles from southern Spain, many of whom had fled to the Barbary states. Later, from the early 17th century onwards, an increasing number of them were European renegades; for instance, by the 1630s more than half of the privateering captains based in Algiers were either European renegades or the sons they had sired locally. The captains of ships of the rulers' own fleets were drawn from the same range of backgrounds. This is hardly surprising, as for the most part these vessels too were simply privateers owned by the ruler himself.

In Algiers, as in the other Barbary ports, the captains tended to maintain houses in the western part of the city, close to the kasbah, with their crews quartered close by. This was a precaution against any attack by political or domestic opponents, and it helped to ensure that the community of privateers formed an identifiable political and social bloc in the city. Once at sea, the privateer captains either operated independently, or

Khizr Barbarossa (c.1478–1576), also referred to by the honorific Hayreddin or Kheir ed-Din (meaning approximately 'the Best'), was the formidable leader of the Barbary pirates for a major part of the 16th century. During his career he juggled his own privateering activities with the governorship of Algiers and military service to the Ottoman sultan.

served together in a squadron or fleet commanded by the Capudan Pasha or one of his appointed deputies. The result was an administrative and command structure that would not have been out of place in the navy of any contemporary maritime state.

It is worth noting that for the most part the leaders of the Barbary pirates were privateers themselves, who had worked their way up into positions of authority through hard-won experience, naval skills and a certain amount of luck. There was no real conflict of interest when these men were summoned to participate in expeditions on behalf of the Ottoman sultan, or even to command his fleets. After all, most of the English 'sea dogs' of the same period were equally adept at combining privateering careers with service to the state – Sir Francis Drake and Khizr Barbarossa were not as dissimilar as one might imagine. Similarly, dedicated Ottoman warships might be deployed to take part in privateering ventures under a Barbary commander, just as Ottoman troops and artillery were used to augment the fighting potential of Barbary warships. Even the janissaries serving in the regencies were regularly detached to provide a core of experienced troops aboard privateering vessels.

The gifted Italian-born Barbary privateer leader Uluç Ali (or 'Ochialli') served under Turgut Reis before rising to become the Beylerbey of Algiers in his turn. He commanded the Barbary contingent at the battle of Lepanto (1571), and three years later he recaptured Tunis from the Spanish.

Dual command

On the frequent occasions when janissaries were embarked a dual system of command was maintained. The reis was in sole command of his ship and crew, but not of the embarked detachment of janissaries. Although they were the hard-core fighting element aboard they remained detached from the normal routine of the ship, only springing into action when an attack was launched. They were commanded not by the reis but by their own *agha* ('officer'), taking orders only from him. While this dual command might

TURGUT REIS AT BATTLE OF PREVEZA, 1538

1: Turgut Reis
This impression, based partly on posthumous depictions, imagines Turgut Reis fighting surrounded by his pirates and janissaries at the battle of Preveza, where, serving as deputy to Khizr Barbarossa in command of the Ottoman reserve, he reportedly turned the tide of battle when he boarded and captured a Papal flagship. At this date the Greek-born captain was 53 years old, described as tall, bearded, and a charismatic leader. He wears the long, buttoned coat and kaftan typical of a holder of senior Ottoman rank, over armour – almost certainly a composite of mail with small plates covering the torso, which was frequently worn either under or sandwiched between layers of fabric. The scabbard of his wide-bladed *yataghan* is thrust under his silk sash.

2: Berber officer
Based partly upon a 17th-century painting by Pier Francisco Mola which shows a senior warrior sporting a slung leopard-skin. His robes are tucked up to allow freedom of movement at sea, and he is armed with a *kilij* sword and a Turkish *agfa* dagger.

3: Hafsid Berber soldier
By contrast, note the enveloping North African arrangement of this man's turban, and his straight broadsword.

4: Janissaries
By this date these elite Turkish infantry soldiers traditionally led boarding parties, fighting both with muskets and swords (the hatchet carried in his sash by the soldier at the right was not intended as a weapon, but to cut up lead ingots for bullet-moulding). Janissaries wore uniform coats in a number of colours (red, blue and green seem to have been common), with the front skirts tucked up in battle; the long 'stand-and-fall' white fabric headdress with a brass headband had a removable frontal tube to hold feather plumes on ceremonial occasions. *Esprit de corps* was important, and they often displayed on their hands tattoos particular to their *orta* (regiment). The weapons are taken from surviving Turkish examples, although the extant matchlocks are of rather later date; powder and priming flasks were often made from rams' horns.

appear problematic (after all, without the agha's consent the ship would not be able to launch an attack or a raid), in practice it seemed to work well enough, and there are no recorded instances of any real conflict. Interestingly, a similar system existed in Spanish warships of the period, but with the difference that the military commander actually took control of the ship during an attack.

Dividing the spoils

Once the ship returned to port any prizes, plunder and captives were dealt with following long-established custom. The sale of ships, cargo and slaves, and the ransoming of prisoners, were managed by the state authorities, who also administered the disbursement of the profits. A previously agreed portion of the gross value – anything from one-fifth to one-eighth – went to the ruler of the regency. Next, other customary deductions were made, to cover the fees of the customs officials, the slave-merchants, the cargo- or

TURGUT REIS (1485–1565)

Turgut (or Dragut) was a Greek-born slave who had converted to Islam and joined the Ottoman army as a gunner. By 1520 he had turned up in Algiers, where he joined Barbarossa's privateers – no doubt being welcomed for his specialist military skill. He soon rose to command his own vessel, and then a squadron of galiots, with which he preyed on Spanish and Italian shipping in the Tyrrhenian Sea and around the coasts of Sicily.

He then moved to the Peloponnese, where he employed small *barca longas* and *fustas* to attack passing Venetian ships. Most notably, in May 1533 his flotilla fell upon two well-armed Venetian galleys of the Cretan squadron as they were patrolling off the Saronic Islands almost within sight of the crumbling walls of Athens. He was equally successful in a major fleet action in 1538, when he commanded the Turkish reserve under Barbarossa at the battle of Preveza (see Plate F). At the climax of the battle he darted forward with two galiots and, at the head of his janissaries, boarded and took the Papal flagship commanded by the Tuscan warrior-cleric Gimbattista Dovizi. In 1540 Turgut Reis became the *Bey* of the pirate lair of Djerba off the Tunisian coast, and thereafter spent several years leading raids in the Central Mediterranean. These included his temporary capture of the island of Gozo, when most of the population were taken away as slaves, and similar attacks around the Tyrrhenian Sea.

Turgut faced his greatest challenge in October 1550, when Andrea Doria appeared off Djerba with a much stronger fleet of Genoese and Spanish galleys.

Turgut's ships were trapped inside the lagoon, and only a small battery covering the narrow Cantera Channel stood between them and the enemy. Knowing that he would be unable to prevent Doria from landing troops to take this last obstacle, Turgut planned a daring escape. He greased the hulls of his vessels, and constructed a greased plank slipway across the sandspit that linked Djerba to the mainland. Under cover of darkness during three successive nights, Turgut spirited his fleet away across the sandspit and into a channel dug through the shallows to deeper waters to the east. Not only did he escape Doria's trap, but on his way to safety he captured two Christian galleys which were on their way to reinforce Doria's fleet.

The following year Turgut surpassed even this achievement when, reinforced by a Turkish galley fleet, he not only recaptured Djerba but also took Tripoli from the Knights of St John. Turgut was named *Bey* of Tripoli, and later *Beylerbey* of Algiers. He went on to defeat Doria in 1552 in a galley fight at Ponza off Naples, and in May 1560 in an even greater battle off Djerba. The Christians had just captured that island, but were unprepared when Piali Pasha and Turgut arrived; they achieved victory within a few hours, and Andrea Doria was one of the few senior Christian commanders to escape.

The two Muslim commanders' next campaign was notably less successful: at the head of a corsair contingent during the great Ottoman siege of Malta in 1565, Turgut was killed before Fort St Elmo at Valetta. His body was taken to Tripoli for burial.

HISTORIE
van
BARBARYEN,
En des zelfs
ZEE - ROOVERS

This illustration from a 17th-century Dutch work promoting the work of the Redemptionist Fathers shows, on the right, an imposing *agha* of janissaries. The Christian prior holds bags of coins; the urgency of his mission of mercy is emphasized (bottom centre) by the depiction of a slave in the stocks having the soles of his feet beaten in the notorious *bastinado* punishment.

ship-brokers, as well as other sums for the upkeep of the port or for its *marabouts* (religious teachers).

The money that remained was divided in two. One half went to the shipowners, either individuals or a consortium of financial backers (the owner was often the ruler himself, or the Capudan Pasha). The other half was divided amongst the crew. Once again, this division of spoils followed long-established rules. First, bonuses were issued as rewards – for instance, to the sailor who had spotted the prize in the first place, or to the first man to board it. The net sum was then divided into several hundred shares, depending on the size of the crew, and issued according to an established ratio. Thus, the captain would get 40 shares, other officers 10–20 shares, sailors 3 shares, janissaries 1½ shares and boys a single share. If the privateer vessel was crewed by former Christian converts, they too shared in the profit, receiving 3 shares apiece like any Muslim sailor.

THE CREWS

The captain of a ship was assisted by a number of officers. These included a pilot to assist with navigation; a sailmaster to supervise working under sail; a chief boatswain to assist him in other aspects of seamanship, and to oversee discipline; a chief gunner to deal with the ordnance; a *khodja* (purser) to supervise the stores and plunder; and, where necessary, an overseer of slaves. There was also the agha of janissaries, as noted above.

The crew themselves were often a complete mixture of men of different ages, races and even religions. There is a lack of hard evidence on the composition of crews (no crew lists survive), so we have to rely on the testimony of witnesses such as Luis del Marmol-Carvajal, a Spanish sailor who was captured by Moroccan pirates and spent almost eight years as a slave on their galleys. Nicolo Carraciolo, the Bishop of Catana, was captured by Turgut Reis in 1561 and wrote about his experience on his release, as did several other clerics. They commented in particular on European renegades in the pirate ranks, the majority of them being English or Dutch, although French and Genoese were also mentioned.

A Barbary pirate, from an 18th-century engraving. His costume seems less unrealistic than most Western depictions of such men, and matches the scant descriptions of their appearance that have survived.

The Muslim members of the crew called all Christians, even their shipmates, 'Franks'. A sizeable number of sailors were Ottoman Turks, usually from either the Adriatic coast or the Aegean basin, while a handful were from Ottoman possessions in Asia Minor or Syria. The final group were natives of the North African coast, mainly Moorish refugees from Spain or former Moriscos, but also some Berbers.

A list of privateer captains operating from Algiers during the 1580s gives an idea of just how varied the pirates' origins were. The list gives the

MURAD REIS (c. 1570–c. 1641)

In late June 1631 a small squadron of 'Sallee Rovers' led by a captain named Murad Reis slipped into Roaring Water Bay on the coast of Ireland's County Cork, and landed near the little village of Baltimore. Pouncing on the sleeping village, they seized 107 men, women and children and dragged them away to be sold as slaves. Reportedly, only two of these unfortunates ever returned home from North Africa. This was Murad Reis's only notable exploit, and he owes his inclusion here solely to the fact that he was actually a Dutchman named Jan Janszoon, from Haarlem.

This privateer turned pirate had arrived in Algiers in 1618, converting to Islam and joining up with other European renegades. By 1619 he had moved to Salé, where he was one of a group of captains who in 1624 proclaimed the port a republic independent of the Moroccan sultanate. For a while he was 'president' of this pirate mini-state, but internal quarrels obliged him to return to Algiers. From there he launched cruises beyond the now-depleted Mediterranean, and in 1627 he ventured as far north as Iceland, though that raid garnered only a dozen captives. He also operated in the Irish Sea and the Bristol Channel; while claims that he established a base on Lundy Island are probably untrue, he certainly harried shipping bound for Bristol in the late 1620s. After the Baltimore raid he operated in the Western Mediterranean for three years, until his capture by a Maltese galley in 1635. After five years as a prisoner at Valetta he managed to make an escape to Tunis, dying in Morocco the following year.

names and original nationalities of 35 men; ten are recorded as being Turks, and six as Genoese. Of the others, three were Greeks, two Venetians, two Spaniards, two Albanians, and one man each from Sicily, Calabria, Naples, France, Hungary and Corsica. One Jewish captain was listed, and three who were the sons of Christian renegades. (Further information on this group is obscured by the habit of giving Muslim names to European renegades upon their conversion to Islam.)

While a few saw privateering as a temporary occupation, most pursued the corso as a career, and when asked gave their occupation as *corsaro* or professional corsair. Almost all were experienced seamen and veteran fighters – captains could afford to select the very best men. A pirate galley or sailing vessel might be a melting-pot of seamen from different backgrounds, but all were united by the common goal of making money. If the venture was successful all would gain from it, and this provided a considerable incentive to work together despite cultural or linguistic differences. According to European writers, these differences were largely overcome by the adoption of a Barbary patois that was used ashore as well as at sea. The basis of this *lingua franca* was the Berber tongue, but it also involved a mixture of Arabic, Andalusian, Italian and some other European words.

European renegades

The presence of so many Europeans in pirate crews is striking. This development probably began in the mid 16th century, when most of the 'Franks' who served in privateers were of Greek, Italian or Spanish descent. At first most of these were seamen who had been captured, and opted to escape slavery by joining the crew and converting to Islam. This ceremony was carried out in port, administered by the *imam* of the mosque frequented by the privateers, or even by the city's mufti himself. The supplicant had to swear to abide by the will of Allah, and was presented with white cloth to make a turban, before being led off to be circumcised. For the most part these converts were welcomed, particularly if they were experienced sailors, or had useful maritime trades such

OPPOSITE
Contemporary depictions of Barbary pirates are rare, but some Dutch maritime artists were known for their attention to detail, so this portion of a painting by Cornelis Hendriksz Vroom may be useful. It shows a Barbary galley sinking after an action with a Spanish warship; the soldiers on and under the frame of the stern-canopy are depicted wearing red, green and brown coats, while the rowers at the right are naked apart from short white trousers.

as carpentry, gunnery or sailmaking. Such men were deemed 'sea ar[...]' a[...] were given positions commensurate with their skills.

Later, a growing number of Christian pirates were lured to the Barb[...] Coast by the prospect of plunder, or the chance to escape from the authori[...] in Europe. One of these men was John Ward, a former Elizabethan privat[...] who was pressed into English naval service in 1603. He promptly deserted in a small sailing craft, taking several others with him. After a brief piratical spree in the English Channel he headed into the Mediterranean, where he continued his pirate cruise. In 1605 he appeared in Salé, where his band was augmented by other European renegades, and the piracy continued. Two years later he moved his operation to Tunis, using the port as his base until 1622, when he retired from his piratical career. Ward was unusual in that when he arrived on the Barbary Coast he already had his own ship and crew. In 1608 the English ambassador in Venice provided an unflattering description of him: 'John Ward, commonly called Captain Ward, is about 55 years of age, very short, with little hair, and that quite white, bald in front, swarthy face and beard. Speaks little, and almost always swearing. Drunk from morn to night. Most prodigal and plucky. Sleeps a great deal…' If Ward was one of the elite of the European renegades, it doesn't say much for the other members of his community.

Three English pirates, pictured during a hard-drinking night out in Algiers (see Plate G). Many former English privateers turned to outright piracy after the end of the war with Spain in 1604, and operated out of the Barbary ports. (From 17th-century reprint of De Nicolay's *Les Quatres Premiers Livres de Navigations Orientales*, 1568)

This comment about drinking chimes with observations made in Barbary itself. These 'Franks' were seen as a race apart, abiding by their own rules. In 1606 the Sieur de Brèves, a French nobleman, wrote: 'The great profit that the English bring to the country, their profuse liberality and the excessive debauches in which they spend their money before leaving the town and returning to war (this they call their brigandage on the sea) has made them cherished by the janissaries of all other nations. They carry their swords at their side, they run drunk through the town … they sleep with the wives of the Moors … in brief every kind of debauchery and unchecked licence is permitted to them.' This misbehaviour was tolerated because these men were needed; they were skilled seamen, and often had a better knowledge of technical matters than was usual in the Mediterranean. Just as importantly, they provided fresh manpower to a privateering fleet based on a coast that lacked either a large population or a strong tradition of long-range seafaring.

Galley slaves

The main difference between Barbary galiots and larger galleys (see above, 'The Ships') was that the smaller vessels

...re almost always crewed by free men. The oarsmen were not shackled slaves, so they could pick up a scimitar, dagger or musket and take part in boarding action. On galleys, however, the rowers were invariably slaves, just as they were in Christian galleys. While this reduced the number of men who could fight, and demanded constant vigilance of the rowing benches, Christian slaves were in relatively plentiful supply and could easily be replaced.

Life as a galley slave was horrendous. The men lived, worked and slept chained to their benches, and all human waste was simply allowed to lie beneath them in the well of the rowing deck. Occasionally the decks were hosed down with sea water, but slave galleys were notoriously noxious; while they looked elegant, contemporary observers claimed that they could be smelt from half a mile away.

The only respite tended to come at night, when the galley put into a sheltered cove, or when the vessel was under sail alone. The slaves were still kept chained, almost always naked, unkempt, and often suffering from malnutrition, exposure, or the attention of the overseer's whip. By contrast, Christian slaves who served in Barbary sailing vessels went unfettered most of the time, so that they could climb the rigging and move around the ship; they were only shackled or locked below decks if an action was imminent. Of course, any hint of rebellion could easily lead to a beating or – worse – being transferred to a galley. Conversion usually brought freedom, and if they were experienced mariners then they could join a pirate crew and share in the plunder. It says much for the power of religion during this period that many preferred to endure a living hell at the oars rather than renounce their faith.

In stark contrast, this 17th-century engraving shows Christian slaves, whose appearance recalls the memoirs of captives who served on galleys, attempting to escape from the Barbary Coast in a small open boat rigged with a makeshift mast and sail. (Illustration from contemporary Dutch history of the Barbary states)

Janissaries

This colourful Turkish depiction of a galley is part of a work commemorating the siege of Famagusta (1570–71). Of equal interest are the Turkish soldiers on the shore, including a contingent of janissaries (right) wearing coats of blue, green and red. The galley is depicted as all red, including the oars, apart from the upperworks at the stern in ochre or pale natural wood. The stern canopy is shown as blue inside, and red with white or yellow patterning outside. The flags are parti-coloured red and black.

The other major element of a privateering crew were the janissaries. A full-sized galley could carry as many as 100 to 140 of these soldiers, while smaller galiots or sailing craft carried proportionately fewer. Not all Barbary privateers carried janissaries (their deployment was at the whim of the Bey de Camp and the Capudan Pasha), but all galleys and most galiots did. As already noted, they took no part in the working of the ship; their job was simply to fight. The janissaries were symbolic of the close relationship between the Barbary rulers and the Ottoman sultan. In the Turkish armies the janissaries, conscripted as boys from Christian populations to be converted and trained, were prized as a highly disciplined elite infantry corps. They were intensely loyal to the sultan, and their courage, professionalism and *esprit de corps* set them apart from most soldiers of the period, both in Asia and in Europe. They could fight with bow or musket, but just as easily as shock troops, charging home with swords and round shields; this naturally made them particularly useful at sea.

The first janissaries to arrive on the Barbary Coast were sent directly from Turkey, and formed part of the troops used to conquer the Berber states in the name of the sultan. They stayed behind to help maintain order, and to safeguard the regencies from internal or external threats. These Turkish soldiers served until death or retirement, and were replaced by a provincial *ocak* (corps) recruited either in the Middle East or even from among the ranks of southern European renegades. While the quality of these provincial recruits has been questioned, few doubted the ability of the janissary officers to turn them into prime soldiers. Service brought valuable

G EUROPEAN RENEGADES, c. 1620

In the early 17th century a growing number of European 'renegadoes' – pirates who were willing to convert to Islam in return for a secure base of operations – made their way to the Barbary Coast. They were welcomed for their skills – for example, in handling square-rigged ships, and gunnery – but earned a reputation for drunkenness and wild behaviour. Under the disapproving eyes of a Turkish official (left), the three main figures here are based upon an engraving from a 17th century reprint of N. de Nicolay's *Les Quatres Premiers Livres de Navigations Orientales,* first published in 1568, which shows three drunkards (probably Englishmen) squabbling over their last flask of liquor during a 'run ashore' in Algiers. Two of them **(1 & 3)** wear a mixture of Turkish and North African garb, including the odd but apparently popular slashed hood-like cap. **(2)** retains largely European clothing, though with the white turban marking him as a Muslim convert; his Germanic dagger is perhaps a souvenir of former employment as a mercenary.

(4) A *Kuloghi* arquebusier, one of the levies of part-Turkish parentage who served the Barbary rulers in return for exemption from taxation. While they were principally cavalrymen they did sometimes serve as gate guards, though they were forbidden from entering the city itself.

(5) The mounted Berber warriors in the background are based on the *Codice de Trajes* (1547), which shows them armed with long, flexible lances, straight broadswords, and straight daggers fastened to their left forearms. Tapestries commemorating the Emperor Charles V's conquest of Tunis in 1535 show them in action.

privileges, and a swaggering superiority over the inhabitants of the Barbary regencies. Janissaries enjoyed high social status, comfortable barracks with slaves attending to their needs, good pay and good food. They were also allowed to make money on the side by pursuing a trade when they were off duty.

In return they were expected to fight, unquestioningly and unflinchingly. They had three principal duties. One was to take part in expeditions into the interior, to gather the annual tribute or to subdue unruly Berber or Bedouin tribes. Another was to garrison the cities and ports of the regencies, to serve their artillery and defend their walls, and generally to maintain the security of the state. This also involved ensuring the security of the regent himself (or at least, when janissary officers were not involved in plotting a coup against him – which was why the inner sanctum of the ruler's kasbah was usually protected by independently recruited palace guards). Their third duty was to serve at sea, and this was a popular assignment: not only did it mean they were actively fighting their Christian foes, but they also directly profited from a share of the plunder.

Detail from a highly stylized 16th-century woodcut showing a Barbary galley in the midst of a sea battle; note, in the centre, janissary archers shown standing on the *arrumbada* platform above the heavy ordnance.

What seemed to amaze observers was the ease with which these diverse Barbary pirate crews could co-exist in relative harmony. According to Luis del Marmol-Carvajal, quarrels were rare, despite the presence of soldiers who did not work the ship, crewmen and gunners from widely differing backgrounds, and slaves whose only escape was death or conversion. This co-operative atmosphere may have owed something to the fact that cruises by galiots and galleys were of reasonably short duration, often little more than two to three weeks.

In the centre foreground of this detail from a painting by Matteo Perez d'Aleccio, showing a scene during the great siege of Malta (1565), red-coated Turkish janissaries await the order to assault the Christian fortifications.

TECHNIQUES & TACTICS

Limitations

A number of factors limited the timing and duration of a privateering cruise, particularly by a galley. Cruises were limited to the period from mid-spring to late autumn; during the winter months the Western Mediterranean is prone to storms, particularly along the coast of the Maghreb and in the Gulf of Sirte. Galleys and galiots tended to make their first sorties in April after wintering in Algiers, Tunis, Tripoli or Djerba.

The other limiting factor was their ability to remain at sea. A galley or galiot had a lot of men crammed into a small, narrow hull, and there was little spare room for water or provisions. The minimum daily water requirement in the hot Mediterranean summer is estimated to have been about 90 gallons per galley per day, and a galley's storage capacity to have been 1,800 gallons, or enough for 20 days.

Barbary pirate galiots, pictured in action against Christian galleys or galiots off the north-east coast of Sicily in a mid 17th-century watercolour by the English sailor Edward Barlow. Amid the billowing clouds of gunsmoke the Barbary vessels are distinguishable by their black and red pennants; their opponents are shown flying the white-cross-on-red of the Knights of Malta.

This was no particular problem if a galley was operating on its own. The Western Mediterranean coast offered many secluded bays where streams or springs could be used to replenish water supplies. Indeed, Piri Reis – the nephew of Kemal Reis – produced a folio of maps of the Mediterranean coast marked with suitable watering-places. But if ships were operating as part of a larger squadron or even a fleet, most inlets offered insufficient concealment, and it took a dangerously long time to fill all the barrels from a single water source. The same was true of provisions: while the crew of a single galiot could put in somewhere and kill a few goats, this was not an option for a larger force. Another limitation of oared vessels was that they had to put in somewhere safe at night. This was one reason why the Spanish developed a string of fortified bases running along the North African coast, as the Venetians did on the Adriatic and Peloponnesian coasts.

For Barbary privateers there was no such luxury once they left their own coast, so they tended to establish temporary bases further afield. For example, in the Tyrrhenian Sea small islands like Stromboli, Ustica, Gigilio, Montecristo, Ponza and Palmarola were all used as watering points and temporary refuges.

H

BARCA LONGAS, EARLY 17th CENTURY

1: The barca longa (foreground) was one of the smallest craft used by Barbary privateers. These light coastal vessels, commonly found throughout the Western and Central Mediterranean, were widely employed by pirates as well as small traders and fishermen. They carried one or two short masts, and while the rig varied according to local customs all were capable of being powered by oars as well as sails. The victim in the centre of this scene, loosely based on a contemporary engraving, is a smaller Sicilian fishing boat powered by a small gaff-rigged sail and oars; interestingly, its rowers face forwards and use inboard-mounted rowlocks. Beyond it a second Barbary barca longa is closing in to cut off any chance of escape, while a small swivel gun mounted on the bow of the nearer vessel is fired across the quarry's bows

to encourage it to heave to. The sail patterns on the Barbary vessels are taken from contemporary illustrations, as are the red and black taffeta flags flown by the pirates.

2a: Example of large 17th-century galley under sail, with square-rigged mainmast but a large lateen yard and sail lying along the deck.

2b: Northern European caravels were potential prey for 16th-century corsairs; this example has square-rigged main and foremasts and a lateen on the mizzen. The caravel was built in a range of sizes and was immensely versatile.

2c: (Not to scale) Small two-masted caravel with lateen rig. Recent research even suggests that Columbus's *Nina* may have been lateen-rigged at some stage.

1

2a

2b

2c

Other islands used in this way included Lampedusa and Pantellaria between Tunis and Sicily; Vacca, off the southern coast of Sardinia; Formentara in the Balearic Islands; and Îles d'Hyères off the French Riviera. Once again, these were practical for one or two vessels or even a small squadron, but not for a whole galley fleet. All these limitations – the need to replenish water and provisions, and to find secure overnight anchorages – became exponentially worse with each extra galley. The larger the fleet, the shorter its range of operation, and so the more limited its operational options.

Despite this, the Barbary pirates certainly put large groups of ships to sea. The largest of the Barbary fleets was that based in Algiers; it was estimated that as many as 50 galleys and galiots were based there in the mid 16th century, and occasionally these would operate together if summoned to do so by one of the great leaders such as Khizr Barbarossa, Turgut Reis or Uluç Ali. More usually, however, galleys or galliots hunted singly or (more commonly) in pairs, and sometimes in small squadrons of between three and six vessels. Interestingly, the figures for the mid 1620s tell a very different story: by then only six galleys were operating out of Algiers, but the port was also home to about 60 large sailing privateers and 40 smaller ones. At the same time Tunis had 34 pirate craft based in its harbour, but Tripoli less than half a dozen, all of them sailing vessels. This shows a general decline in numbers of galleys, particularly in the two smaller ports, and a steady increase in the number of sailing vessels used for privateering.

Hunting-grounds and prey

Having left port, either sailing alone or with a consort or two, a typical privateering galiot would set a course for one of its favoured hunting-grounds, which often depended on the vessel's home base. Algerine pirates tended to head towards either the Strait of Gibraltar or the Balearic Islands. From the Strait they could range out along the Atlantic coast of Spain and Portugal; from the Balearics they could sweep clockwise around the Western Mediterranean, towards Sardinia, Corsica and the southern coast of France. If this did not produce enough profit they could enter the Tyrrhenian Sea and cruise off the west coast of Italy. Privateers based in Tunis tended to operate in the Tyrrhenian Sea and off either coast of Sardinia or Corsica, or else headed east past Malta to cruise the Central Mediterranean south of Crete. The Tripoli corsairs preferred to operate around Sicily, particularly the eastern coast, where shipping passed through the bottleneck of the <s>Strait</s> of Messina. Alternatively they could follow their colleagues from Tunis <s>and</s> operate south of Crete, hoping to snap up Christian trading ships bound <s>for</s> the Levant.

The shipping these pirates preyed upon was subject to the vagaries of the marketplace and of the political situation in Europe, but they tended to follow long-established trade routes. The leading ports of the Western Mediterranean – Valencia, Barcelona, Marseilles, Genoa, Naples, Palermo, Messina and Syracuse – all relied on coastal trade linking them together, and were also the termini of longer sea routes running between Sicily or Italy and Spain, passing to the south of Sardinia. To the east, Venice dominated trade in the Central Mediterranean, and much of this passed through waters within the Ottoman sphere of influence – the Aegean Sea, or along the southern coast of Asia Minor to the Levant.

The 17th century saw the growth of trade between northern Europe and the Mediterranean, and by the middle of the century the Levantine trade was almost wholly dominated by the Dutch and English. By that time (the end of our period) privateering was complicated by the signing of individual treaties with the Barbary states that involved the payment of 'protection money'. Venetian merchants claimed that these arrangements favoured the Dutch and the English: by such means the northerners' ships became immune to pirate attacks, which was cited as one of the reasons for the decline in Venetian trade during the century.

Battle tactics

The Barbary pirate captain was essentially a slave-hunter – to him, taking a ship at sea was less about material plunder than the capture of the crew. Similarly, they could achieve the same ends by raiding the coast of a Christian country. As already noted, such attacks were usually carried out by no more than a handful of vessels, their combined crews being counted in the low hundreds rather than the thousands. It was only when summoned to join an Ottoman fleet for a specific campaign that larger numbers of Barbary vessels were grouped into fleets manned by thousands of fighting men. The captives taken then would be far more numerous than the usual score or so of seamen and villagers; this level of force allowed the attackers to raid larger ports, or to range further inland to attack unsuspecting towns several miles from the sea. By the 16th century a string of small lookout towers already dotted the Christian coasts of the Western Mediterranean, where many of them can still be seen today. These might give the locals some warning of a raid, and thus a chance to flee inland.

Occasionally, pirates – particularly the 'Sallee Rovers' from Morocco's Atlantic coast – would sweep as far north as the British Isles or, on one notable occasion, the coast of Iceland, but most raids were confined to the Mediterranean coasts of Spain, France and Italy. During larger raids it was common to seize a town as a defensible forward base, from which to launch expeditions inland. While Christian accounts complain about the looting of churches (including their bronze bells, presumably for Barbary gun-foundries), most smaller raids involved a stealthy nocturnal attack, the throwing of a cordon around a village, and then a systematic search for potential slaves. As the 16th century wore on some coastlines actually became depopulated as villagers and farmers moved inland for safety. Larger villages and towns were fortified, and a mutual defence system was created so that troops could respond quickly to help the locals resist raiders. In the 1/ century some pirates even complained about the lack of human prey; or expedition encountered no potential captives apart from two yout.s swimming off a beach and a small boat manned by a pair of fishermen.

This scarcity of victims was less of a problem at sea, as the waters of the Western and Central Mediterranean remained busy throughout the period, and the business of hunting for prizes was reasonably straightforward. First, the privateers had to spot a potential victim; this could be done either by a lookout stationed at the masthead, or else from the high ground of an island lair. (In 1504, when Oruç Reis attacked the Papal flagship, he had posted lookouts on high ground on the island of Elba.) The privateers then shot out from behind the cover of a headland and caught the passing ship unawares. These 'ambush sites' were particularly useful in places where shipping had to pass through a bottleneck, such as the waters between Corsica and Sardinia, the Strait of Messina, or the passage between Sicily and Cape Bon. When the Spanish writer Miguel de Cervantes was captured by Barbary pirates in 1575 he noted that his captors beached their prizes in a secluded bay on the coast of the French Camargue, presumably a favoured hiding-place because its marshes made for difficult access from inland.

It was said that once Barbary pirates sighted a prize it was already doomed to capture, which reflected the edge in speed that they usually enjoyed over a lumbering merchant ship. Barbary sailing vessels were noted for carrying more sail than other ships of their size, while galleys and galiots were careened between cruises – about once every two months– to keep their lower hulls free of weed and barnacles. When this was done the pirates also coated the lower hull with wax to make it slide through the water more easily. Typically, a galley could make up to 8 knots under sail (9½mph/14kph).

A Barbary pirate galiot (left) and galley (right) take on a well-armed Spanish merchant ship, in this early 17th-century painting by an unknown Spanish artist. In reality the pirates would do their utmost to avoid the broadside guns of their adversary as they closed with it.

The mid 17th century might have brought the golden age of the Barbary pirates to an end, but they continued to prey on shipping intermittently for more than another 150 years. This early 19th-century watercolour shows a privateering frigate, with only the flag of Algiers to distinguish it from a contemporary European warship.

While a good rowing speed was about half that, practised and highly motivated oarsmen could propel a galley at up to 12 knots (14mph / 22kph) for short bursts, until the rowers grew too tired to keep up the pace. Here the pirates had an edge over other galleys, because if slaves were used captains were able to select them from among prime seamen, used to hard conditions and to rowing.

To lure their prey within range Barbary corsairs would often dress as Christian seamen, keeping their distinctive janissaries hidden and flying false colours. This long-established pirate trick could be surprisingly effective. In 1665, Le Sieur de Chastelet des Boyes described his capture by a vessel powered by both sail and oar, its flags 'covered with crescents, suns and stars'. It fled when a group of six new vessels appeared, flying Dutch flags. The French ship headed towards these craft: 'But alas, as soon as we were within musket shot the Dutch flags disappeared, and the masts and the poops were simultaneously shaded by flags of taffeta of all colours, enriched and embroidered with stars, crescents, suns, crossed swords and other devices and writings unknown.'

He added that the Barbary flagship was well armed, and opened fire on his vessel. For most privateers the aim was to persuade the victim to surrender without putting up a fight, so as they closed in they would usually fire guns as a warning. If this did not bring about an immediate surrender the pirate ship would close fast, her decks lined with men making as much noise as possible – yelling abuse, firing muskets, banging drums, blowing trumpets, and beating the side of their ship with the flat of their swords. (In De Chastelet's case he heard them shouting 'Brébé, mena pero!' – 'Surrender, dogs!') If the pirate vessel were a galley or galiot then it would run its raised prow close alongside the merchantman's hull and fire swivel guns across its decks before the pirates boarded. If available, janissaries would lead the attack, armed either with their muskets or wielding sword and shield. Few European crews were willing to stand up to them in a fight, and most boarding actions ended quickly with the defenders throwing down their weapons.

There were exceptions, however. English and Dutch seamen were more likely to resist than the crews of Mediterranean vessels, and the northern European ships in those waters tended to be larger and better armed than many others. It was believed that a spirited defence using the ship's broadside guns would usually persuade most Barbary pirates to go off in search of easier prey. Sometimes, however, these larger roundships were becalmed, or overwhelmed by sheer weight of numbers. If surrender was inevitable some crews were known to take to the boats after setting fire to their ship, or laying a fuse to the magazine, to deny their attackers the prize.

Once a prize was captured, the pirates – again, led by the janissaries – would search the vessel for plunder, as well as the passengers and crew. Obviously wealthy passengers or officers were particularly sought after, as they could be ransomed for large sums. Servants or seamen were less lucrative, and would inevitably find themselves taken to the slave-markets when the pirates returned to port. If capture seemed inevitable the victims would often swallow their money, the rich would exchange clothes with their servants (perhaps a foolish move), and men would hide their valuables where they could. The pirates were wise to these tricks, and examined their captives closely; the hands and the teeth were the best indications of rank and status, while beating or the administration of a salt-water emetic would usually result in the retrieval of hidden or swallowed money. There are very few accounts of women prisoners being mistreated by Barbary pirates. The janissaries were under strict orders to protect female captives, and the sailors followed their lead. However, like the male prisoners, they were now destined to be sold as slaves in the marketplaces of Salé, Algiers, Tunis or Tripoli.

If the prize was a galley, Muslim slaves would immediately be freed, while Christian captives – the former crew – would be chained at the oars in their place. Once the pirates had gathered enough captives or taken enough prizes

Christian captives being landed on the harbour front of a Barbary port, presumably Algiers, in one of a series of 17th-century engravings depicting the plight of Christian slaves. While much of the scene may be fanciful, it highlights the very real importance of slaves to the Barbary economy right up to the 19th century.

turned to port. Their arrival was usually a triumphant affair, with flags
guns fired in celebration, and onlookers flocking to the shore to see
itest crop of Christian slaves being unloaded. For all the attempts of the
ian powers to put the pirates out of business, this scene would be
r ed on the Barbary Coast not only throughout our period, but also as
late as the early 19th century.

FURTHER READING

Bradford, Ernle, *The Sultan's Admiral* (London; Hodder & Stoughton, 1968)

Crowley, Robert, *Empires of the Sea: The Final Battle for the Mediterranean 1521–1580* (Faber & Faber Ltd; London, 2008)

Dearden, Seton, *A Nest of Corsairs: The Fighting Karamanlis of the Barbary Coast* (John Murray; London, 1976)

Earle, Peter, *Corsairs of Malta and Barbary* (Sidgwick & Jackson Ltd; London, 1970)

Falconer, William, *Falconer's Marine Dictionary* (David & Charles; Newton Abbot, 1970. Reprint of original first published in 1769)

Gardiner, Robert (ed), *Cogs, Caravels and Galleons: The Sailing Ship 1000–1650* (Conway Maritime Press; London, 1994)

Gardiner, Robert (ed), *The Age of the Galley: Mediterranean Oared Vessels since Pre-Classical Times* (Conway Maritime Press; London, 1995)

Guilmartin Jr., John F., *Gunpowder and Galleys: Changing Technology and Mediterranean Warfare at Sea in the Sixteenth Century* (Cambridge University Press; Cambridge, 1980)

Guilmartin Jr., John F., *Galleons and Galleys* (Cassell; London, 2002)

Heers, Jacques, *The Barbary Corsairs: Warfare in the Mediterranean, 1480–1580* (Greenhill Books; London, 2003). First published as *Les Barbaresques: La course et la guerre en Mediterranée, XIV–XVI siècle* (Editions Perrin; Paris, 2001)

Jamieson, Alan G., *Lords of the Sea: A History of the Barbary Corsairs* (Reaktion Books Ltd; London, 2012)

Kempf, Peter (ed), *The Oxford Companion of Ships and the Sea* (Oxford University Press; Oxford, 1976)

Konstam, Angus, *Renaissance War Galley 1470–1590*, New Vanguard 62 (Osprey Publishing; Oxford, 2002)

Landström, Björn, *The Ship: An Illustrated History* (Interpublishing AB; Stockholm, 1961)

Lloyd, Christopher, *English Corsairs on the Barbary Coast* (Collins; London, 1981)

Malcolm, Noel, *Agents of Empire: Knights, Corsairs, Jesuits and Spies in the Sixteenth Century Mediterranean World* (Allen Lane; London, 2015)

Marquardt, Karl Heinz, *Eighteenth-Century Rigs & Rigging* (Conway Maritime Press; London, 1992)

Platt, Richard, 'Corsairs of the Mediterranean' in Cordingly, David (ed) *Pirates* (Turner Publishing Ltd; Atlanta, GA, 1996)

Rogers, William L., *Naval Warfare under Oars, 4th to 16th Centuries: A Study of Tactics, Strategy and Ship Design* (Naval Institute Press; Annapolis, MD, 1967)

Tenenti, Alberto, *Piracy and the Decline of Venice, 1580–1615* (Longmans, Green & Co Ltd; London, 1967)

Tinniswood, Adrian, *Pirates of Barbary: Corsairs, Conquests and Captivity in the 17th-Century Mediterranean* (Jonathan Cape; London, 2010)

INDEX

Note: page numbers in bold refer to illustrations, captions and plates. All weapons and equipment are US.